Robert Schuler

Four Ways of Modern Poetry

Four
Ways
of Modern
Poetry

EDITED BY NATHAN A. SCOTT, JR.

 JOHN KNOX PRESS
RICHMOND, VIRGINIA

To Harvey and Lucy Shaw

CONTENTS

EDITOR'S INTRODUCTION

A few years ago at a birthday dinner for the late Robert Frost in New York at which Lionel Trilling was the speaker of the evening, Mr. Trilling scandalized his audience by calling Frost "a terrifying poet." He denied that Frost "controverts the bitter modern astonishment at the nature of human life" or that he "reassures us by his affirmation of old virtues, simplicities, pieties, and ways of feeling . . ." Indeed, said Mr. Trilling, "the universe that he conceives is a terrifying universe": he declared Frost's enormous distinction to consist in the great clarity with which his poetry has "made plain . . . the terrible things of human life," and he suggested that this may be why Frost can be so deeply loved, since "only a poet who [can] make plain the terrible things [can] possibly give [us] comfort."[1]

But the beautiful tribute that he paid the great old "Sophoclean" provoked—to his surprise, and mine—cries of outrage and indignation in the press a few days later, for apparently more people than one would have supposed wanted to preserve in their minds the conven-

---

[1] Mr. Trilling's address is now available most conveniently in *Robert Frost: A Collection of Critical Essays,* ed. by James M. Cox (Englewood Cliffs, N. J.: Prentice-Hall, Inc., 1962), where it is published under the title "A Speech on Robert Frost: A Cultural Episode."

tionally pleasant image of Frost as the tartly garrulous old celebrant of the Arcadian landscape of New England hills and snow and meadows and woods. Yet, for all of the angry opposition that was offered to his testimony, Mr. Trilling was telling the essential truth, and Frost *is* a terrifying poet, as Professor Elmen is here at pains to remind us in his essay on Frost's "design of darkness." And, indeed, it is precisely the candor with which they render "the terrible things of human life" that makes the three other writers to whom this book is devoted exemplary figures, along with Frost, in the poetry of our time. For the great poets of the modern period, "like St. George, [have] gone out to capture dragons."[2] The extraordinary richness and distinction of their work is in large part an affair of the radicalism with which they have faced into the "boundary-situations" of human existence in an age when "all is in doubt, all coherence gone." And though their "stays against confusion" have not often been found in the great inherited traditions of religious belief, they do not for this reason lose authenticity of relevance to modern sensibilities: indeed, that authenticity may itself in part be proved by the audaciousness with which new terms for the Sacred are conceived or with which the old terms are drastically reconceived.

The scale of the series of books to which this volume belongs has imposed the most stringent limitations of scope; and, as a consequence, it has been impossible even to attempt here the kind of spaciousness of view

---

[2] Stanley R. Hopper, "The Problem of Moral Isolation in Contemporary Literature," in *Spiritual Problems in Contemporary Literature,* ed. by Stanley Romaine Hopper (New York: Harper & Brothers, 1952), p. 154.

which is in fact asked for by the rich diversity in the poetic art of our time. But, nevertheless, thinking that it might be useful—particularly for college and university students—to provide for a Christian response to some of the focal bodies of this literature, John Knox Press invited me to organize a little symposium that would express something of what may be entailed in this response. And I am grateful both to the Press for the original proposal and to my collaborators for their prompt and generous helpfulness.

My essay on W. H. Auden is a very much briefer and a very considerably revised version of an essay ("The Poetry of Auden") which first appeared in *The Chicago Review* (Vol. XIII, No. 4; Winter 1959) and then later in *The London Magazine* (Vol. VIII, No. 1; January 1961). Thanks are herewith tendered to the editors of these journals for their willingness to allow the republication, in altered form, of this material; and thanks are also to be tendered to the publishers who have permitted the use of quotations from the copyrighted works of Wallace Stevens, Robert Frost, Dylan Thomas, and W. H. Auden.

N. A. S., Jr.
University of Chicago
8 April 1965

I *Wallace Stevens:*

THE SUNDRY COMFORTS OF THE SUN

BY STANLEY ROMAINE HOPPER

> His self and the sun were one
> And his poems, although makings of his self,
> Were no less makings of the sun.[1]

The poetry of Wallace Stevens is a solar poetry. The above lines—in which the self, the sun, and the poems are ingenuously instated one within the other—contain the Alpha and Omega of his vision. The later poems glow in a gold redundancy of the sun. He seems always to have been seeking

> The heraldic center of the world
> Of blue, blue sleek with a hundred chins,
> The amorist Adjective aflame . . . (172)

This is, in fact, what the poems of Stevens are about: they are the data of his quest for the heraldic center of reality and for the deep center of his own psyche.

This amorist Adjective aflame is not the traditional God of Christendom. It is no longer possible for the poet to think or compose against the background of "some outer patron and imaginer" (O.P. 109). For Stevens

13

> The heaven of Europe is empty, like a Schloss
> Abandoned because of taxes.... (53)

It is the same in Jersey City: "The steeples are empty and so are the people ..." (210).

This sense of the dropping away of the entire symbolic world of Christendom is radical in Stevens; hence his perpetual pursuit of "candor" (382), "integrity" (36), and the "accurate tongue" (509). Because the "attributes with which we vested, once, the golden forms" (317) are there no longer, we are destitute: our "paradise of meaning" has ceased to be and we inhabit a time of "lustred nothingness" (320). We are at the point of radical need, and

>   ... we require
> Another chant, an incantation, as in
> Another and later genesis ... (321)

The controlling themes for Stevens' work as a whole are present already in the central poems of *Harmonium*.

In "The Comedian as the Letter C" his aesthetic hero, Crispin, has already left the old world to seek a newer continent in which to dwell. There he aims

>   to drive away
> The shadow of his fellows from the skies,
> And, from their stale intelligence released,
> To make a new intelligence prevail. (17)

In his early masterpiece, his "Sunday Morning," Stevens' aesthetic heroine explores the rift between the world that has dropped away and the distress which overtakes us in the ebb of former meanings.

Why should she give her bounty to the dead? . . .

.   .   .   .   .   .

Shall she not find in comforts of the sun
Things to be cherished like the thought of heaven? (67)

This appeal to the comforts of the sun, as against the
decline of traditional Christian forms, is based upon the
premise that divinity must be within the world as given,
not superimposed from above or deferred to some remote and static Paradise into which we enter after death.
Stevens (at this stage) rejects the ancient myths. At the
same time he visualizes a "ring of men" chanting

Their boisterous devotion to the sun,
Not as a god, but as a god might be,
Naked among them, like a savage source.
Their chant shall be a chant of paradise,
Out of their blood, returning to the sky . . . (70)

This is clearly a ritual under the sun. But is the sun the
"heraldic center" of that ring of chanting men? With the
demise of the structures of Christendom, we stand between the times, bereft of the honored consolations,
holding the tessellated sunlight in our hands.

In this early period Stevens also became open, in part
at least, to depth recognitions:

A loud, large water
Bubbles up in the night and drowns the crickets' sound.
It is a declaration, a primitive ecstasy,
Truth's favors sonorously exhibited. (321)

The accurate tongue must know these favors in the midst
of its acceptance of the blunt reality.

The greatest poverty is not to live
In a physical world. . . .

The green corn gleams and the metaphysicals
Lie sprawling in majors of the August heat,
The rotund emotions, paradise unknown.
This is the thesis scrivened in delight,
The reverberating psalm, the right chorale. (325-326)

The accurate tongue has its rootage in the soil of earth's particulars; but it must "make the bread of faithful speech" (408), and it must know the cadence of "the right chorale."

The failure of literary criticism generally to adduce the Stevens secret is due in large measure to its failure to move from the sharply etched surfaces of the poems to the deep quest of the poet himself—his search for "the bouquet of being," the "poem of pure reality, untouched /By trope or deviation . . ." (471).

The poet plays upon an instrument, whether Harmonium or Blue Guitar, eliciting the opulent chord or the "black fugatos" (507), reaching through "the banjo's twang" (393) for truth's favors sonorously exhibited, for the poem behind the poems, the poem of pure reality, the rhythms of the right chorale. But Stevens also knows the point where the reach of the instrument fails:

I cannot bring a world quite round,
Although I patch it as I can . . . (165)

At the same time, the poem succeeds precisely where it fails. "Poetry is a pheasant disappearing in the brush," he wrote in his *Adagia* (O.P. 177). The poem is neither the pheasant nor the disappearance of the pheasant: it is the movement itself, *the pheasant disappearing*, the mystery of the moment of becoming in the lacunae *between* being and becoming, actuality and possibility, day and night, sun and moon, masculine and feminine, reality and imagination. The poem is a conspiracy of metaphor and propositional severance so contrived as to capture in the noose of recognition that evanescent whole which is ineluctably more than the sum of its parts, but which leaves the parts precisely what they are. The poem *occurs* at the point of intersection where the dynamic opposites contained in the chosen scope or cosmos of the poem's postulations meet and choir or orchestrate together. The poem *happens* at the point where reality as given is disappearing into the underbrush of its own possibilities. Reality is rescued from the fixations of its own clichés, or from its vagabondage toward the lassitudes of everydayness. "Poetry is a renovation of experience" (O.P. 177). It is "a happening/ In space and the self, that touched them both at once . . ." (483). In short

> The poem is the cry of its occasion,
> Part of the res itself and not about it. (473)

The word "occasion," as it is used here, should be understood in Whitehead's sense—the philosopher who, along with Santayana, is most congenial to Stevens' way of seeing things. The occasion is at once a specific entity and a novel happening. It is at once immediate and ultimate. In Whitehead's terms:

> The ultimate metaphysical principle is the advance from disjunction to conjunction, creating a novel entity other than the entities given in disjunction. The novel entity is at once the togetherness of the 'many' which it finds, and also it is one among the disjunctive 'many' which it leaves; it is a novel entity, disjunctively among the many entities which it synthe-

sizes. The many become one, and are increased by
one. In their natures, entities are disjunctively
'many' in *process of passage* into conjunctive unity.[2]
What does this mean as applied to poetry? It is exem-
plified perfectly by Stevens' "Anecdote of the Jar":

> I placed a jar in Tennessee,
> And round it was, upon a hill.
> It made the slovenly wilderness
> Surround that hill.
>
> The wilderness rose up to it,
> And sprawled around, no longer wild.
> The jar was round upon the ground
> And tall and of a port in air.
>
> It took dominion everywhere.
> The jar was gray and bare.
> It did not give of bird or bush,
> Like nothing else in Tennessee. (76)

This is an early poem; but it is an "anecdote" of all other
poems. It exhibits the way in which the artwork as-
sembles its world about itself and gives order and an
awareness that were not there before. Yet it does so by
being what it is and letting everything else be what it is.
The poem is a "fiction" fabricated by the imagination
which, out of the nothing of its own inner-ness, creates
a novel order and a "meaning" where none was before.
Yet in so doing, the poem, the imagination, "Like light,
. . . adds nothing, except itself" (N.A. 61). He might
just as well have said, "like music," for a page later he is
quoting from Verlaine:

> . . . la mandoline jase,
> Parmi les frissons de brise.[3]

This is the way of "The Man With the Blue Guitar":
which instrument, out of nothing, adds that resonance of
itself by which the accurate tongue of things as they are
chatters in the vacant wind of circumstance, or rejoices
to the rhythms of the right chorale. Thus

> Poetry
> Exceeding music must take the place
> Of empty heaven and its hymns,
>
> Ourselves in poetry must take their place,
> Even in the chattering of your guitar. (167)

From this point on, the movement of Stevens' poetry
is away from the bright novelties of the ego-conscious-
ness which are mainly masks of our assertiveness by
which we hide ourselves from ourselves. The persistent
revel of his early verse, its "gauds of rhetoric,"[4] its "fru-
gally unified opulence,"[5] its "imperative [but discursive]
haw/Of hum" (28), is put aside. The wit remains,
but it is qualified by the poet's inner quest. The poems are
"abstract," in the sense of modern art; but they begin to
disclose the emergent symmetry of his deeper metaphorical correlations, all having to do with his quest for
"the heraldic center of the world." Three ways appear
(which are at the last one way): the way of wit, the poet
as Comedian, a *via negativa;* the way of metaphor, the
poet as seer, a *via analogia animae;* the way of rapture,
the poet as musician, a *via mysterium coniunctionis.*

The way of wit is typified by Crispin, the comic hero
of our times, who undertakes the voyage to a newer
world. Crispin is at once the poet, seeking ways to make
experience vivid; and western history, whose center has
moved out from under Europe's heritage (Crispin sails

from Bordeaux); and he is also man himself, leaving his projected gods, and coming to himself, to "major man." Crispin's large pretensions make him comical. He is little more than the letter *c*—the "merest minuscule in the gales." Yet his venture is heroic: he leaves the continent of congealed meanings to discover a newer way of seeing things. He sets out upon the seas, "a skinny sailor peering in the sea-glass."

Two motifs are here: Crispin as voyager, and Crispin as comedian-clown.

The *persona* of Crispin as voyager moves in Stevens' poetry into the late Ulysses poems (520, O.P. 99). Also in "Prologues to What Is Possible" the venturing hero experiences "an ease of mind that was like being alone in a boat at sea." It was a boat built of stones that were no longer heavy, like the body of objective knowledge suddenly become vivid. No longer did he feel the dread of "voyaging out of and beyond the familiar." Instead

> . . . he traveled alone, like a man lured on by a syllable without any meaning,
> A syllable of which he felt, with an appointed sureness,
> That it contained the meaning into which he wanted to enter . . .
> As at a point of central arrival . . . (516)

Crispin too had felt "the appointed power," his call to poetry. The "appointed sureness" here confirms the early sense that poetry is a means to renewal, in a time "when the gods have come to an end" (O.P. 209).

But the important turn now follows. It is the turn to himself, into the disclosure of a newer self than he has known, which flick of privilege

> Creates a fresh universe out of nothingness by adding
>   itself,
> The way a look or touch reveals its unexpected magni-
>   tudes. (517)

Thus the Crispinesque voyage is a voyage into the possible. It is also an acceptance of the conditions of voyage
as a continuing journey to ourselves in a world of open-
ness.

Meanwhile the *persona* of Crispin as *comedian-clown*
moves differently. The recurrences of the comedian-
clown imagery are manifold—including the mask, the
masquerade, the circus, the mimics, the marionette, the
manikin, the scarecrow. The forms of wit are precious
here.

> It is with strange malice
> That I distort the world . . . (61)

he says. Poetry, if it is to trick the reader out of his
quotidian world and into transparency, "must resist the
intelligence almost successfully" (350, O.P. 171). "It is
necessary to propose an enigma to the mind," he says
again (O.P. 168, 170). The poems of Stevens are often
nuts to be cracked, or Silenuses to be opened, or rebuses
which yield their meaning only when read with pa-
tience and persistence and meditated below the surfaces
of craft and wordplay. Therefore wit becomes internal
to the function of the poem in "an age of disbelief." The
poem must slip by the patterned expectations of the
time's consciousness much as wit in dreams slips by the
superego's censorship.

The Canon Aspirin (in "Notes Toward a Supreme
Fiction," *It Must Give Pleasure,* v-viii) is still a slightly

comic figure, but he is also an apostle of the possible. He represents the cure for the headaches of our unrealities. He expounds the remedy of wholeness, the trick of which is not to impose, but to discover; so to hear "the luminous melody of proper sound" (404), and know that "I have not but I am and as I am, I am" (405).

Worse, however, then the headaches is the backache of our broken history. The Canon here gives way to Saint John of the Apocalypse. Our western culture, personified as backache, has apotheosized the mind, since it only can defend against itself. But Saint John, unmasking this false primacy, points to the primacy of *Presence*, which fills the self before the mind can think. Presence is the primal mystery. "The world is presence and not force" (436). Nor is it mind. It arises from "most incredible depths." "I speak," the poet in Saint John remarks, "below the tension of the lyre" (437). And quite surprisingly, at this point, the artifices of wit (and the poet as Comedian) have petitioned the poet as Musician: but, still more surprisingly, in a vision of a new apocalypse, the saint perceives "the possible nest in the invisible tree" (437), and we are already in another set of metaphorical correlations—those of the poet as seer.

The way of the seer is a way of centering. It is, as a matter of fact, an extension of the "anecdote" of the "Jar in Tennessee": which, as a visual representation of higher and lower relationships, is duplicated in Stevens' image of the tree and in his image of the rock. Like the jar at the top of the mountain, Stevens also sees

> ... a tree that bears
> A semblance to the thing I have in mind.
> It stands gigantic, with a certain tip

> To which all birds come sometime in their time.
> But when they go that tip still tips the tree. (17)

The symbol of the rock, which is an emergent symbol, is invariably pictured as a mountain

> . . . half way green and then,
> The other immeasurable half, such rock
> As placid air becomes . . . (375)

It is always green or covered with leaves or blossoming below and always gray and bare as it thrusts into the upper sun. It "cannot be broken. It is the truth" (375). Stevens' final book of poems is called "The Rock." The rock is an obvious symbol of that movement of "centering" that we see throughout his poems. Yet, in "The Rock," we are told that we must be "cured" of it (and of the ground, and of ourselves). What does this mean?

Two clues are provided. The first, in "Credences of Summer" (373), supplies the missing term. Here is depicted "the final mountain," and on its top a tower— "the natural tower of all the world . . . Axis of everything": underneath the gold sun. "This is the center that I seek." The jar, the tree, the tower, the mountain (the sun?), have merged with the world's axis! The figuration of the rock or mountain stands for the goal of the self's pilgrimage, and has the psychological meaning of the Self.

If we return now to Saint John's vision of the possible nest in the invisible tree, another dimension is added. For this is the tree

> Which in a composite season, *now unknown,*
> *Denied, dismissed,* may hold a serpent. . . .
> Whose venom and whose wisdom will be one. . . . (437)

This is the serpent of Asklepios (which often dwelt in

trees), and which is therefore a serpent of possible heal-
ing. Asklepios, the divine physician, combined light and
helpfulness in his person. He was primarily Apollonian,
of the sun. Nevertheless his beginnings were from a union
in the chthonic world, and hence the cure he brings com-
bines the "below" and the "above" into a unity. The figure of the serpent is not a frequent one in Stevens'
poetry; but it is significant that the opening invocation,
in "The Auroras of Autumn" (in some respects Stevens'
greatest poem), is addressed to the serpent of Asklepios.

This will help us to understand why, in the poems on
"The Rock," it is "not enough to cover the rock with
leaves" (poems).

> We must be cured of it by a cure of the ground
> Or a cure of ourselves . . . (526)

Yet *if* these poems broke into bloom and bore fruit, they
"might" be a cure of the ground. They would then become an icon, a sacred image of being, the figuration of
blessedness,

> . . . a cure of the ground and of ourselves,
> In the predicate that there is nothing else. (527)

The symbols of stone, diamond, mountain, rock, do often function as symbols of the self, and represent the
solidity and permanence of a psyche that can no longer
be split apart by the tension and the tug of opposites.
One feels, however, that the jar, the tree, the tower, and
the rock exhibit, in Stevens, a phallic incompleteness
yearning for its union with "the heraldic center of the
world."

The poet must learn to "solemnize the secretive sylla-
bles" (420); through our images it is

> As if, as if, as if the disparate halves
> Of things were waiting in a betrothal known
> To none, awaiting espousal to the sound
>
> Of right joining, a music of ideas, the burning
> And breeding and bearing birth in harmony,
> The final relation, the marriage of the rest. (464-465)

It is here that the poet approaches that rapture in which the poet as musician comes to know within the poem's utterance (logos)—his *via mysterium coniunctionis.*

This is the rapture of the right chorale. It is also "the little ignorance that is everything" (the cure proposed by Saint John for the backache of our fallen history). It is, religiously speaking, the moment of union with God.

The term "God" is appropriate here only, perhaps, in Stevens' revised sense of Presence, and in the further sense that the search for the "centre"—especially the centre within a circle—is, psychologically, a figuration of the nature of God. What Stevens seeks to exclude is the patterned thinking of "that gold self aloft," a projection of ourselves, which, by being named, imposes our own dichotomies upon ourselves and is divisive like a feud that has forgotten its own origin. His invocation to the sun (in his "Notes Toward a Supreme Fiction," It Must Be Abstract, I) contains the first premise of his theology:

> The sun
> Must bear no name, gold flourisher, but be
> In the difficulty of what it is to be. (381)

This is a radical immanence of Being, known or unveiled or unconcealed (Heidegger) to us only in the discreet occasions of its passage into conjunctive unities—which it is the task of the poet to announce. This can be done for Stevens only in the "idiom of the work," the idiom of innocence—"not [in the idiom] of the enigma of the guilty dream" (which is, I take it, the Christian doctrine of sin and the Fall). While there is never a *place* of innocence, there may always be a time of innocence: it exists almost as pure principle, almost a predicate of things. The aurora borealis, which flames and flares like a Heraclitean fire upon the horizons of our awareness, is not malicious but benign:

> ... these lights are not a spell of light,
> A saying out of a cloud, but innocence.
> An innocence of the earth and no false sign
>
> Or symbol of malice. That we partake thereof,
> Lie down like children in this holiness,
> As if, awake, we lay in the quiet of sleep,
> As if the innocent mother sang in the dark
> Of the room and on an accordion, half-heard,
> Created the time and place in which we breathed ...
>   (419)

This is an arrival. It is a dwelling in the heart of life's mysteries, which it is the purpose of Stevens' poetry to celebrate. It is a moment of wholeness, a circle with a center, the self surrounded by the auroras of Being. The corolla of opposites opens into plenitude; at the same time the innocent "mother" sings in the dark and we lie down like children in this holiness. The "mother" also is a poet: her music on the accordion creates the time and place of our occasion. The archetype of the poet as musician is thus a summation symbol.

The accordion has something in common with Stevens' first symbolic instrument, the harmonium, which was a small organ played on a keyboard when air was forced by a bellows through a series of metallic reeds. There was humor in this image: it fit the bravura and self-consciousness of Stevens' early poetry, much of which seemed forced by the bellows of his manifest and romping talent.

Then came the blue guitar, suggested by Picasso's painting and suited admirably to the poet's purpose and theory:

> They said, "You have a blue guitar,
> You do not play things as they are."
>
> The man replied, "Things as they are
> Are changed upon the blue guitar."
>
> And they said then, "But play, you must,
> A tune beyond us, yet ourselves,
>
> A tune upon the blue guitar
> Of things exactly as they are." (165)

The poet's instrumentality—through his fictions, on the guitar—changes things as they are into their latent possibilities; in like manner, to see things as they really are the self must be changed into what it really is. But what it is is nothing static. It must stand within the music of its own becoming.

I have argued elsewhere that if the rock is taken as Stevens' metaphor of metaphors, and the poem taken as the icon of this barren (solar) centering, then the icon remains outside the center and its report is hollow, like the box of the blue guitar; that what the poet twangs or figures is but the wistful-witful "tom-tom, c'est moi" of our rational dialectic thumping on the drum of man's fantastic consciousness. The rock images taken alone, untutored by the flocculence of other image correlations in the poetry, leave us bound to the hard core of earth's "gray particular." Does Stevens remain chained, like Prometheus, to this chthonic mother defying the solar tyrant with his abstract cries? Or is there in this rock a Silenus hidden which, like the rocks and caves of antique lore, awaits the talisman (the magic Word) to open and release the locked-in treasure?

Surprisingly enough, Stevens himself provides a clue in "The Rock" (Part I). Here, looking back over his seventy years, it seems to him almost absurd to think that "the sounds of the guitar," or the miraculous "meeting at noon" of lovers, could possibly have been: and yet they were—"*As if nothingness contained a métier*" (526). *The box* of the blue guitar is precisely that nothingness. It is the drum of emptiness which provides that resonance without which the strings would not resound and the possible Presence come to its occasion. The universe that Stevens cannot find a center in is itself that box of the guitar whose emptiness becomes a Presence when we play things as they are. Likewise with the deep Self, not to be grasped by definition: its nothingness becomes a resonance of Being in the world of beings when it responds to the logos coming to expression from the heart of things. The poem behind the poems is in the poem unconcealed. And poetry, as Gerhart Hauptmann has remarked, is the art of letting the Word resound behind the words. This also is a cure of the ground and of ourselves.

Was Stevens aware that in his break away from "the rotted names" (183) he had himself petitioned a most ancient incantatory form? When called upon to perform a cure the Tremyugan shaman (or medicine man) always began by beating his drum and playing his guitar as a means of inducing ecstasy. Then the shaman would make his journey into the underworld to bargain for the soul of his patient. His descent began by a journey to a mountain, symbol of the Cosmic Axis at the "Center of the World."[7] If "poetry/ Exceeding music must take the place/ Of empty heaven and its hymns," it is not surprising that poetry in Stevens assumes a priestly office and must undertake the journeys to the underworld on our behalf; but since the underworlds are now for us archaic (save as archetypes of the Unconscious), the journey has become for us a journey into nothingness. It is not surprising that the poet clings in spite of himself to the rock of "mind" and does not wish to risk the venture into nothingness.

By the same token the blue guitar remained for Stevens a frivolous symbol; so he turned to the lyre, as Rilke did, and sought to know that Presence below the tensions of the strings. The lyre also dropped away. Then, at last! in "Credences of Summer" (376) the long-awaited instrument appeared!

> The trumpet of morning blows in the clouds and through
> The sky. . . .
>   The trumpet cries
> This is the successor of the invisible.
>
> This is the substitute in stratagems
> Of the spirit. This, in sight and memory,
> Must take its place, as what is possible
> Replaces what is not. The resounding cry
> Is like ten thousand tumblers tumbling down

> To share the day. The trumpet supposes that
> A mind exists, aware of division, aware
> Of its cry as clarion, its diction's way . . . (376–377)

Thenceforth we stand "in the tumult of a festival" (415), in the idiom of innocence: for the poet has become the herald of the always Alpha of becoming, the messenger of belief beyond "belief," announcing that from the throats of nothingness the trumpet calls of creation's possibilities resound. "The prologues are over. It is a question now, / Of final belief" (O.P. 250).

Thus, at the end of his life and work, it was possible for Stevens to affirm that:

> His self and the sun were one
> And his poems, although makings of his self,
> Were no less makings of the sun.

Crispin had begun as a fagot in the lunar fire; he became a new resemblance in the sun. To his claim that the poem "is the cry of its occasion" his work bears witness. That its occasion might well be a slight one (a poet's immortality is brief) he knew quite well, as with the "scrawny cry" he heard in the early dawn at winter's end. It was a lone bird's call:

> That scrawny cry—it was
> A chorister whose c preceded the choir.
> It was a part of the colossal sun,
>
> Surrounded by its choral rings . . . (534)

Thus the little comedian as the letter c persists to the end: but all the archetypes of Stevens' work are gathered in its cry. It is a herald, a forerunner of the choral trumpet of the sun—that colossal sun surrounded by its trumpet rings, like Dante's choir about the throne of Cod. This also is the box of Being resonant with praise, the amorist Adjective aflame with Alpha's always dawning of surprise.

NOTES

1. "The Plant on the Table," from *The Rock;* in *The Collected Poems of Wallace Stevens* (New York: Alfred A. Knopf, 1954), p. 532. Numbers in parentheses throughout indicate page references from this edition. Citations from Stevens' *Opus Posthumous* (New York: Alfred A. Knopf, 1957) are indicated as O.P.; and citations from *The Necessary Angel: Essays on Reality and the Imagination* (New York: Alfred A. Knopf, 1951) are noted as N.A. Used by permission of the publisher.
2. *Process and Reality: An Essay in Cosmology* (New York: The Macmillan Company, 1929), p. 32, italics mine. Cf. "A Primitive Like an Orb," *Collected Poems,* pp. 440-443.
3. . . . . . . the mandolin chatters
   In the shiverings of the wind.
4. R. P Blackmur, *The Double Agent: Essays in Craft and Elucidation* (New York: Arrow Editions, 1935), p. 93.
5. Marianne Moore, *Predilections* (New York: Viking Press, 1955), p. 34.
6. "Reports and Prophecies in the Literature of Our Time," *The Christian Scholar,* Vol. XL, No. 4 (December 1957), p. 318.
7. Mircea Eliade, *Shamanism: Archaic Techniques of Ecstasy,* tr. from the French by Willard R. Trask (New York: Pantheon Books, Inc., 1964; Bollingen Series LXXVI), pp. 220-224.

II *Robert Frost:*

THE DESIGN OF DARKNESS

BY PAUL ELMEN

The poetry of Robert Frost is loved by readers all over the world, even though the fashionable critical taste may find it bland and sentimental. Readers who listen only to the counsel of their hearts remember much of his verse gratefully:

> Something there is that doesn't love a wall,
> That sends the frozen-ground-swell under it,
> And spills the upper boulders in the sun. (47)[1]

Actually the lines only seem to be simple, and owe their memorable quality to an unimaginable complexity. Robert Frost has his own richness, which should assure his fame amongst the devotees of ambiguity: unanswered questions concealed by a surface lucidity, a sense of the ceremony of words pretending to be plain and un-studied, a deep sense of peril masked by a hopeful smile.

All of these qualities are visible in "Stopping by Woods on a Snowy Evening," one of the poems which the audience always asked for when Frost was "barding around" the lecture circuit:

> Whose woods these are I think I know.
> His house is in the village though;

He will not see me stopping here
To watch his woods fill up with snow.

My little horse must think it queer
To stop without a farmhouse near
Between the woods and frozen lake
The darkest evening of the year.

He gives his harness bells a shake
To ask if there is some mistake.
The only other sound's the sweep
Of easy wind and downy flake.

The woods are lovely, dark and deep,
But I have promises to keep,
And miles to go before I sleep,
And miles to go before I sleep. (275)

Most of the distinctive notes in Robert Frost's singing voice are in this poem. What perhaps strikes us first of all is that the details seem taken from life, rather than being imitated from other poets. In distinction from much modern poetry, the ideas are simple, the language conversational. They seem to have been written by an uncomplicated man who was so sure of himself that he did not need to pose; no modern poet would dare to begin a poem with unashamed banality, "Whose woods these are I think I know." The tone is not accidental. Frost was fascinated by speech patterns—the shape of words as they fell from the mouth—and many of his poems make us think of a local sage sitting next to the pickle barrel in a country store and telling his cronies what he said to some summer folk. As his friend the English poet Edward Thomas wrote to Gordon Bottomley in 1915, "All [he] insists on is what he finds in all poets—absolute fidelity to the posture which the voice assumes in the most expressive intimate speech." Like a Crawford Notch Wordsworth he listened carefully to the lilt and snap of his neighbors' voices. And at his best he approached the lyrical magic of Wordsworth, setting down a simple utterance which is at once commonplace and astonishing, a preconceptual gavotte like the leap of a faun:

> I'm going out to clean the pasture spring;
> I'll only stop to rake the leaves away
> (And wait to watch the water clear, I may):
> I sha'n't be gone long.—You come too. (1)

"Stopping by Woods" displays the speaking voice of a New England farmer. Its visual detail is also brushed in from life, and not improvised or copied from books. Only an extraordinary city slicker knows that a horse would obey an order to stop at an empty field in an evening during winter, but would shake his bells with impatience at the novelty of the whole enterprise. No summer visitor, Frost always wrote of rural matters like a man who lived in the country, selecting with confidence the detail which would call up a sharp image before the reader's eye. "Blue-Butterfly Day" could well have been written by a man holding a piece of straw in his mouth. Frost's butterflies sit in the road like

> flowers that fly and all but sing:
> And now from having ridden out desire
> They lie closed over in the wind and cling
> Where wheels have freshly sliced the April mire. (277)

The disarming quality of Frost's verse which helps it to find a way into our hearts is that the artifice is concealed, and we have the impression of seeing the people

and places of New England through the eyes of a New
Englander. There is always the vast good humor of a
spinner of yarns who enjoys what he is doing because
he knows he does it well. Describing an old man's winter night, he makes us feel for the moment that we also
are old and alone on a night in winter, with strange
sounds everywhere:

> And having scared the cellar under him
> In clomping here, he scared it once again
> In clomping off . . . (135)

The naïveté is of course not that at all, but an ex-
quisite manipulation carried off so smoothly that you
never notice the poet's fine Spanish hand. A close com-
parison would be Picasso's childlike line. In middle life
Frost wrote,

> It was a cord of maple, cut and split
> And piled—and measured, four by four by eight,
> And not another like it could I see. (126)

And in old age his eye for visual detail had not failed:

> The winter owl banked just in time to pass
> And save herself from breaking window glass.
> And her wings straining suddenly aspread
> Caught color from the last of evening red
> In a display of underdown and quill.
> To glassed-in children at the winter sill. (I.C. 63)

He seemed all his life what he appeared to be on the lecture platform: a Yankee farmer whose eyes were gen-
tian blue and whose pursed lips could talk the sun down
before anyone was bored. He was Heidegger's authentic
man. He seemed like a cultivated peasant, one of Frans
Hals's happy rustics who had somehow had a classical

education. He seemed anachronistic, one of the last of the frontier folk who could deal directly with a real universe and who could speak their minds plainly with no trace of *arrière-pensée*.

An accurate report on the sights and sounds of the world around him is one of the hallmarks of Frost's poetry. But there is another quality which appears in his verse: a suggestion of a hidden depth which the surface of nature imperfectly conceals. The obscure power appears sometimes as a benign and beckoning mystery and sometimes as a vaguely threatening form. In "Stopping by Woods" the traveler is attracted to the sight of the falling snow, but this is not why he stops; the deep, dark woods beckon seductively toward an unspeakable simplicity like the tedium of the grave, from which he is rescued only by recollecting his human bonds. In the woods, particularly as night falls, one can feel a strange presence like a Druid crouching behind a megalithic stone.

Frost was a habitual nightwalker, and several of his poems report incidents from his nocturnal rambles. Even when he lived in Boston he walked at night around Beacon Hill, stopping to toss coins into the schoolyard for some child to find, and into the Back Bay in imitation of George Washington. He loved the dark but he loved it as one who respected its mysterious power. "Storm Fear" develops the familiar theme:

> When the wind works against us in the dark,
> And pelts with snow
> The lower chamber window on the east,
> And whispers with a sort of stifled bark,

> The beast,
> 'Come out! Come out!'—
> It costs no inward struggle not to go,
> Ah, no! (13)

But again it is only the thought of his human duties which saves him.

What lay in the surrounding darkness? What was hidden by the veil of matter? If there were a presence hidden in the night, could it not destroy us? It is something more than his way of speaking when he reports that all out-of-doors looked darkly in at the old man on the winter night. In "Design," he finds a moth killed by a white spider lying in wait in a white flower that normally is blue:

> What had the flower to do with being white,
> The wayward blue and innocent heal-all?
> What brought the kindred spider to that height,
> Then steered the white moth thither in the night?
> What but design of darkness to appall?—
> If design govern in a thing so small. (396)

The last lines suggested a problem which troubled Frost during his lifetime: Is there meaning in the universe? Do even the minor events in time and place have reference to a plan which is greater than themselves? Does the darkness have design? In one of his last poems, "Accidentally on Purpose," he says that he studied the sky to see if the universe

> had the purpose from the first
> To produce purpose . . . (I.C. 34)

If he could be sure that there was purpose in the universe, he would not quibble about the attributes of God, or the worship proper to Him. Never mind "whose purpose" ruled the world:

> Grant me intention, purpose, and design—
> That's near enough for me to the Divine. (I.C. 34)

Search the sky as he would, there was no reply granted him. He was very sensitive to the charge which critics sometimes brought against him, that he was only a shrewd observer of the surface of life. When he looked into the well, they said, he saw only a Whitmanesque reflection:

> Me myself in the summer heaven godlike
> Looking out of a wreath of fern and cloud puffs. (276)

But if he did not see more, it was not for lack of trying. Once, he said, once he had actually seen something more:

> *Once,* when trying with chin against a well-curb,
> I discerned, as I thought, beyond the picture,
> Through the picture, a something white, uncertain,
> Something more of the depths—and then I lost it.
> Water came to rebuke the too clear water.
> One drop fell from a fern, and lo, a ripple
> Shook whatever it was lay there at the bottom,
> Blurred it, blotted it out. What was that whiteness?
> Truth? A pebble of quartz? For once, then, something.
> (276)

The irony expresses the scorn of one who had searched long and hopefully for something beyond sense data, and may actually have seen it; yet of these arcane matters no one could be sure, least of all of those who spoke glibly about supernatural experience.

But the heavy irony is only a temporary mask, because

Frost continued his search for the design in the darkness, and once or twice thought he had succeeded. In "Two Look at Two" he tells about a walk with his wife up the mountainside. Just as they were about to turn back, they saw a doe, and then they saw a buck join the doe. The animal pair and the human pair stared at each other as though they shared some secret understanding:

> Two had seen two, whichever side you spoke from.
> 'This *must* be all.' It was all. Still they stood,
> A great wave from it going over them,
> As if the earth in one unlooked-for favor
> Had made them certain earth returned their love. (283)

The evidence that earth returns the love which man lavishes upon it had by this time been unlooked-for, since the search had for so long been futile; and it was not any evidence which was remembered, since poems after this reveal the same skepticism. What Frost was finally sure of was not the love which the earth might feel, but the love that a man could feel for the world, and also for a fellow human being.

So he consoled himself with the reflection that the presence in the dark wood, drawing the traveler who stops to see the snow fall, is not really there at all. There was a danger in the winter night—the danger, for instance, of the lost traveler in the Alps, who loses his hope and falls asleep in a snowdrift; but there is no presence, except that poets like to say it that way. The something that tears down stone walls is not really elves, of course; what ruins a stone wall is frost and hunters. The most an honest man can admit is that one can act *as if* there were a design in the darkness. He liked to talk about the incident in *Pilgrim's Progress* where Pilgrim is asked, "Do you see yon shining gate?" And Pilgrim replies, "Yes, I *think* I do," and then continues his journey as though he did. In the introduction to Robinson's *King Jasper* (1935), Frost gave expression to his own Hamlet-like mood: "The play's the thing. Play's the thing. All virtue in 'as if.'" Frost loved to play games, but he played them solemnly, as children do.

What need not be banished to a subjunctive limbo was the sensible world with its varied and lovely texture. Though he sometimes felt the danger in the dark, his more normal mood was a vast affection for the people, trees, birds, horses, and insects which appear so vividly in his verse. If he quarreled with the world, he said, it was a lover's quarrel. He liked to read *Walden* and *Robinson Crusoe,* both of which have to do with the wresting of a snug retreat in the center of wildness. Compare the security of Frost's "A Drumlin Woodchuck" with the psychotic anxiety in Kafka's short story "The Burrow." Kafka's animal is trapped by the smallness of his home, while Frost's animal is proud of his tiny retreat "under the farm":

> If I can with confidence say
> That still for another day,
> Or even another year,
> I will be there for you, my dear,
>
> It will be because, though small
> As measured against the All,
> I have been so instinctively thorough
> About my crevice and burrow. (365-366)

The anthology piece "Birches" makes the point that however much he feels like leaving the earth (like the

traveler drawn into the snowy woods), he always ends
by returning gratefully to the solid earth, much as a
swinger of birches climbs away from the ground and
then leaps out and back to the place where he started
from:

> I'd like to get away from earth awhile
> And then come back to it and begin over.
> May no fate willfully misunderstand me
> And half grant what I wish and snatch me away
> Not to return. Earth's the right place for love:
> I don't know where it's likely to go better. (153)

The mock terror ("May no fate . . . snatch me away")
is vintage Frost. His subject is the death-wish which had
haunted him from his earliest years, and which was a
serious threat to his peace of mind. We are surrounded,
he well knew, by darkness; whether that darkness has a
design and is friendly is a serious subject, perhaps the
only serious question. But whenever Frost approaches
what was for him a deeply troubling problem, he plays
the situation for laughs. Some critics have thought this
characteristic lapse of taste, since the prospect of anni-
hilation may be comic in a grotesque and horrifying
way, but is certainly not material for a weak jest. The
terror which is dissipated by such a weak quip is not
terror at all, but only mystery acting "as if" it were terror.
One of his lecture-platform couplets is telling:

> It takes all sorts of in and outdoor schooling,
> To get adapted to my kind of fooling.

Actually he was too sure of the solidity of the visible
world to think very often that it might be destroyed;
and when the thought occurred he banished it with a
cracker-barrel quip:

> We make ourselves a place apart
> Behind light words.

Almost any one of the enchanted lyrics which Frost has left us could be cited to show Frost's love of life's bittersweet meaning, which for him could only be found in a shower of sights and sounds. What caught his fancy one summer day was seeing a fallen meteorite being dragged to a building site on what that particular district called "as stone-boat":

> Some may know what they seek in school and church,
> And why they seek it there; for what I search
> I must go measuring stone walls, perch on perch . . .
> (214)

He knows well that the meteorite which pleases him is only an ordinary star, and not the kind of fabled star which heralded a birth or death. It is the kind of star anyone could see. And yet this proud claim could be made for it, it is a real star and part of Frost's real world, which for better or worse is

> the one world complete in any size
> That I am like to compass, fool or wise. (215)

With some such motivation in mind, the traveler pauses momentarily on the snowy road; he peers with fascination into the darkening wood, thinking how easy it would be to flee from the ambiguities of existence into the simple terror of glory of the darkness; but he clucks to the horse and picks up the icy reins and feels the lurch of the sleigh runners in the rutted road because he is not simply a part of nature, like a stag or a tree, but is a man. Like all men he must not betray his humanity:

But I have promises to keep,
And miles to go before I sleep,
And miles to go before I sleep.

In the end, it was the human community which re-
claimed Frost, and he had fulfilled his promise when he
died at the age of eighty-nine in January 1963. But he
lived in the society of men and walked amongst us
with a difference: he had his circle of light, and his last
book was called *In the Clearing;* but the dark woods were
troubled in the clearing. He seemed a man who cleared
the leaves from the pasture spring knowing that Pan
lurked under the roots of all the trees, and that in a dim
forest glade a child was being sacrificed to Moloch. In
"Acquainted with the Night," which some critics think
is the loveliest lyric in our language, he told us about his
loneliness:

I have been one acquainted with the night.
I have walked out in rain—and back in rain.
I have outwalked the furthest city light. (324)

He hears a cry—but it is from another street, and it is not
for him; he sees the village clock—but the time it
proclaimed was neither wrong nor right. Frost fulfilled
his promise to his fellowmen with a conviction that the
night had a secret meaning which had escaped him.

The sense of life as an enchanted forest which appears now and then as a quixotic element in Frost's lucid
verse may have been due to a vestigial Swedenborgianism which had survived from his childhood days. His
mother, Belle Moodie Frost, had become deeply inter-
ested in the Swedish mystic under the tutelage of the

Reverend John Doughty, whom she had met in San Francisco. Later she sent Robert to a Swedenborgian Sunday school in Salem, New Hampshire. He never formally adopted the exotic doctrine of the Swedenborgians, but it would be very strange if their powerful teaching did not impress the young poet. As a matter of fact, he had at least two mystical experiences in his life: once when he encountered a mysterious figure at the juncture of two roads (he reported the strange event in a letter to Miss Ward on February 10, 1912); and another time when he was walking with Edward Thomas in 1914 (he described the experience twenty years later in "Iris by Night"). He once described himself as "Presbyterian, Unitarian, Swedenborgian, Nothing," suggesting that at one stage of his life he had accepted the teaching and had later given it up. But after the suicide of his son, Carol, in 1940, he said that he had taken great comfort from reading the prophetic works of Swedenborg.

It seems clear that Frost's name must be added to the long list of writers who were influenced by Swedenborg —for example, Coleridge, Blake, Emerson, Carlyle, and the elder Henry James. The idea that there is no separation between the spiritual and the natural world, but on the contrary every object, fact, or phenomenon corresponds to some immaterial idea, must surely be considered one of the influential ideas in the history of western culture. "It is known," wrote Swedenborg with the mystic's calm assurance, "that there is the spiritual and the natural; and that the spirtual flows into the natural, and presents itself to be seen and felt in the forms which fall under the sight and touch" (*The Apocalypse Revealed*, No. 1). In *Divine Love and Wisdom* he re-

ported that he had overheard a remark made to another
spirit by Sir Hans Sloane, who had been in his lifetime a
President of the Royal Society. Sir Hans said, "that if he
had before known what he then knew of the spiritual
world, he would have attributed nothing to nature, except subserviency to the spiritual element . . . as a means
of fixing what continually flows into nature" (No. 344).
The archetypal idea in Swedenborgianism is that the
goodness in anything earthly is an influx from heaven, and
noxious things are influxes from hell. The idea led to a
greatly intensified interest in the empirical world, so that
Swedenborg made important discoveries in anatomy,
astronomy, and engineering, besides having frequent
conversations with people who had entered the spirit
world. The evidence is wanting, but it is possible that
Robert Frost's sensitivity to the world about him was
stimulated by the Swedenborgian doctrine of the materi-
ality of spirit.

There are, however, passages in Frost's poetry which
most certainly are Swedenborgian in background. The
frontispiece of *In the Clearing* says that

> God's own descent
> Into flesh was meant
> As a demonstration
> That the supreme merit
> Lay in risking spirit
> In substantiation.
> Spirit enters flesh
> And for all it's worth
> Charges into earth. . . .

His poem "Kitty Hawk" speaks of the "mighty charge"

> Of the soul's ethereal
> Into the material. (50)

In an article called "Education by Poetry: A Meditative Monologue," which appeared in *The Amherst Graduate Quarterly* in February 1931, Frost made this significant comment: "But it is the height of poetry, the height of all poetic thinking, that attempts to say matter in terms of spirit and spirit in terms of matter. It is wrong to call anyone a materialist simply because he tries to say spirit in terms of matter—as if that were a sin. The only materialist—be he poet, teacher, politician, or statesman—is the man who gets lost in his material without a gathering metaphor to throw it into shape or order. He is the lost soul."[2]

Several critics have pointed out the difficulty of working out a coherent system of beliefs from Frost's poetry, and Yvor Winters gave him an Emersonian title with reverse English: "the spiritual drifter as poet." But it would perhaps be at once more kind and more accurate to see him as a Swedenborgian Yankee. He was of course a Down East type, laconic, independent, addressing philosophical and theological problems with the same common sense he used when the mare dropped a foal. "VURRY Amur'k'n," was Ezra Pound's description of him to Alice Henderson in March 1913, "with, I think, the seeds of grace." Mixed with the horse sense was a strong strain of mysticism, inherited from Swedenborg, which he was never able to accept and never able to reject. And built into his world view was the ability to live with contrast and contradiction, an awareness of life as a point of balance between opposite tugs and stresses.

The total impression one gets from reading Robert Frost is that of a warmly human, perceptive man—the kind of person it would be fun to go haying with, or picking blueberries. His stock of ideas may lack profundity, but they do not lack interest; reading him is a little like a visit to a country store. He shared with most artists a love of the empirical—his world could be touched and heard and seen. Whatever universality he has depends on the fact that he is an authentically regional intellect which deals happily with commonplace themes from the world which lay around him like a farm. "A Prayer in Spring" asks God for pleasure in flowers, in the orchard, in bees, and in birds, only failing when he becomes philosophical: "For this is love and nothing else is love."

Together with this love of the concrete goes another quality which also is familiar among artists: a distrust of the abstract, of the impalpable, of the supernatural. There are no absolute answers in his verse. What we value him for especially, apart from the sheer nostalgic delight of his rural tone, is the delightful aperçu, the momentary flash of intuitive truth which commands our assent. And this is all he wanted from us. "A good poem," he said in the preface to the *Complete Poems* in 1949, "like love, ends in a clarification of life—not necessarily a great clarification, such as sects and cults are founded on, but in a momentary stay against confusion."

Such momentary stays against confusion were old-fashioned qualities like neighborliness, courage in the face of adversity, the ability to keep promises. We shall remember him at the inaugural of President Kennedy, struggling against the wind to read the poor couplets which celebrated the kind of political intransigency which he and President Kennedy both admired:

> There was a book of profile tales declaring
> For the emboldened politicians daring

> To break with followers when in the wrong,
> A healthy independence of the throng,
> A democratic form of right divine
> To rule first answerable to high design . . .
> Firm in our beliefs without dismay
> In any game the nations want to play. (I.C. 30)

These are the qualities which serve as a momentary stay against confusion, or, to use Frost's metaphor, clearings in the forest.

We must be grateful for the richness he has left us, and not accept our gift with a complaint because it was not more. Frost's position is secure in the pantheon of American verse. He had, to be sure, no sustained tragic depth, and he never understood how even the light in the clearing was unsteady because of the surrounding darkness. He was whimsical when his subject matter merited positive conviction, and he should never have risked *A Masque of Reason,* which is a strawberry-festival Job. He should have shunned those ultimate problems which were not his métier, and which made him appear a foxy Grandpa. But when he had his own, proper themes, and when the light was right, he was good, very, very good:

> Sometimes I wander out of beaten ways
> Half looking for the orchid Calypso. (158)

Someone probably had to sing the wonder of dogs, cows, woodchucks, horses, barnyard hens, and hired help. He would perhaps have preferred larger themes, and would have liked a spacious world-view which would have helped him to deal with the great tragic events in his own life. But country folk are not good at pretending, and Frost never paraded a faith he did not feel. His problem was precisely that of the ovenbird, "a mid-summer and mid-wood bird," who is heard only when the season is well advanced and even waning:

> The question that he frames in all but words
> Is what to make of a diminished thing. (150)

What conceivable belief would be a permanent stay against confusion? What is the design in the darkness which is the design also of the clearing? Swedenborg had suggested one answer which appealed greatly to Frost, but which he could not take as his settled position. Yet he snatched from the ominous wood a handful of poems which help us forget for a while the human predicament, and help us for the moment to understand at least some diminished things. And this sad and gentle bard also left us his question: Is there a universal principle, a controlling metaphor, by which the intolerable fullness of the world may be ordered and loved without fear?

NOTES

1. Numbers in parentheses following quotations indicate page numbers in *Complete Poems of Robert Frost*. Copyright 1916, 1921, 1923, 1928, 1930, 1934, 1939 by Holt, Rinehart and Winston, Inc. Copyright 1936, 1944, 1951, © 1956, 1958, 1962 by Robert Frost. Copyright © by Lesley Frost Ballantine. Reprinted by permission of Holt, Rinehart and Winston, Inc. I.C. indicates quotes are from *In the Clearing* by Robert Frost. Copyright © 1956, 1960, 1962 by Robert Frost. Reprinted by permission of Holt, Rinehart and Winston, Inc.
2. All rights reserved. Reprinted by permission of the Estate of Robert Frost and Holt, Rinehart and Winston, Inc.

III *Dylan Thomas:*

POETRY AND PROCESS

BY RALPH J. MILLS, JR.

In English poetry of the first half of this century Dylan Thomas remains one of the unique figures, combining as he does in his work a rich complexity of language and image with an astonishingly pure lyricism. The vision which informs his writing, deepening and maturing throughout his career, places him in line with some of the finest Metaphysical and Romantic poets. Thomas's early poetry is based on certain intuitions about nature, human life, and the relationships between them. These intuitions derive first from the biological side of life, the powerful and persistent sexual impulse urging man to procreate, and the destructive element of time to which he is submitted from the very instant of his conception in the womb. Life circles on a wheel of "process," to employ a word which the poet introduces quite strikingly in his initial book, *18 Poems* (1934), where he describes this paradoxical condition in juxtaposed images of impregnation and death:

> A process in the weather of the heart
> Turns damp to dry; the golden shot
> Storms in the freezing tomb. (6)[1]

Further on in this poem we are told how the climate of life is inescapably of this sort ("A process in the weather of the world/Turns ghost to ghost; each mothered child/Sits in their double shade") (6); and in the well-known "The force that through the green fuse" Thomas renders even more definitely the parallels between the generative/destructive process operating in man and in nature. The poem's first three stanzas are devoted to examples of such correspondences: what creates or nourishes life in nature does so in the poet (or man) as well; what deprives and kills in the natural world will do the same to the poet. Ironically, the creative energy is perceived as identical with the murderous:

> The force that drives the water through the rocks
> Drives my red blood; that dries the mouthing streams
> Turns mine to wax.
> And I am dumb to mouth unto my veins
> How at the mountain spring the same mouth sucks. (10)

The poem ends in lines which again blend figures of the sexual act with those of death and burial. Time begins to undo life at its origin, compelling man, in this poem, to seek an imperishable heaven beyond its domination. Nowhere in his work is Thomas entirely free of this agonizing sense of temporal rule, of the sentence of death to which all are condemned. We will find this awareness just as surely and obviously in "Fern Hill" or "Poem in October" as we do in his earliest verse, but in later poems it is mediated and qualified by a view which is much broader and more inclusive even if it does not stand on any dogmatic certainties.

In reply to various questions about poetry asked by

the magazine *New Verse* in 1934, Thomas remarked that his work was "useful" to him because "it is the record of my individual struggle from darkness towards some measure of light," and added that it should be useful to his readers for a similar reason, for they know "that same struggle." Certainly the atmosphere of the early poems, with their dense, difficult imagery, complicated syntax, and imaginative probing into strange and remote corners of experience, seems to suggest a world forever shadowy and grim, a world where the outcome of any act or gesture, of all love and of each individual life is the final obliteration of death. Thomas explores his themes, most of them dependent upon that understanding of existence as cyclical process, in ways which try to represent the actual *feeling* of process within the composition of the poem. He draws liberally on images rising into consciousness from below the mind's surface; one image is allowed to recall another, and that one another. These are not merely written down when they occur, as in the Surrealist method of automatic writing, but are carefully developed, through many drafts and versions, into the finished poem, for Thomas was a meticulous craftsman. Yet the completed poem, by its fresh and startling arrangement of experience in language, appears to render the immediacy of perceptions and associations hidden from the rational intelligence or from ordinary knowledge.

These early poems, like the remainder of Thomas's work, manage to show considerable variety in spite of persistent themes; and it would be misleading to say that they contain only dire predictions. In "When once the twilight" the poet assumes the voice of a mother who

starts to tell us of her child's birth as if she were witnessing it from within, a not uncommon vantage point with
Thomas. Much of the imagery is borrowed from chemis-
try, engineering, and biology, and gives the impression of
an endless interchange and connection of things in the
universe; elsewhere, as Jacob Korg noted, Thomas por-
trays the universe as a grand machine, process its functioning. The child, in the womb's waters, will be re-
leased gradually, like a ship sent through locks from one
body of water to another (he is also seen as discharged
like a cannon shot a stanza later); time is there too, at-
tending at the birth of its new victim:

> When once the twilight locks no longer
> Locked in the long worm of my finger
> Nor dammed the sea that sped about my fist,
> The mouth of time sucked, like a sponge,
> The milky acid on each hinge,
> And swallowed dry the waters of the breast. (4)

After his birth, the infant is sent out "scouting on the
globe," that is, he enters into the life of the world. But
when he falls asleep his recumbent figure arouses fears in
the mother of death; two subsequent stanzas treat the
subject of mortality:

> All issue armored, of the grave,
> The redhaired cancer still alive,
> The cateracted eyes that filmed their cloth;
> Some dead undid their bushy jaws,
> And bags of blood let out their flies;
> He had by heart the Christ-cross-row of death.
>
> Sleep navigates the tides of time;
> The dry Sargasso of the tomb
> Gives up its dead to such a working sea;

And sleep rolls mute above the beds
Where fishes' food is fed the shades
Who periscope through flowers to the sky. (4-5)

The first stanza here is clear enough in its unpleasant physical details; it implies once more, of course, that at the moment of birth one starts preparing to die. References to Christ's crucifixion (also to a row of cemetery crosses) are not unusual in Thomas's early verse, where they are symbolic of man's fate but in no way promise salvation or resurrection. Christ serves as Everyman for the poet at this stage. Regeneration in these poems occurs merely as a phase of process consisting of rebirth into nature and its continuous cycle, as in the second stanza above. There we also find the floor of the sea, a constant image in Thomas's writing of the kingdom of the dead and thus the source for the more general, as well as more specifically religious or allegorical, type of resurrection described in later poems: "Ceremony After a Fire Raid" or "Ballad of the Long-legged Bait," for example. Thomas follows the Elizabethan poets in linking sleep with death; and the infant, who has left the womb (here a "tomb" to keep up the mortality/process theme), now sets sail on "the tides of time" and presumably gains familiarity with the unconscious as he dreams. Images from the subconscious mediate between man's spiritual being and nature, conveying knowledge of his participation in process; that seems to be what Thomas means. The human individual is doomed by his physical body to decay and death, and so belongs to the world of nature; but his mind or consciousness or spirit is both aware of this destiny and capable of protesting it. In the present poem, however, the mother turns away from

such thoughts and settles for the possibilities which life
has still to offer her newborn son; she calls him to waken
to them as the poem ends:

> The fences of the light are down,
> All but the briskest riders thrown,
> And worlds hang on the trees. (5)

Thomas often brings his poems to conclusion on a similar note of hopefulness, though it is not always so con-
vincing in terms of what has preceded it. Occasionally,
the grim prospects of existence far outweigh any esti-
mates of value the poet can provide. Obsessive sexuality,
the recognition of death growing up in the individual
from the outset, the wheel of natural process which de-
stroys him even while it preserves and renews the
species, the likeness of man's physical make-up to that of
the external cosmos—

> Night in the sockets rounds,
> Like some pitch moon, the limit of the globes;
> Day lights the bone;
> Where no cold is, the skinning gales unpin
> The winter's robes;
> The film of spring is hanging from the lids. (29)

—these recurrent elements in Thomas's work, though
they are by no means visible in every poem, nonetheless
confine his interests and limit his perceptions somewhat.
The best of this poetry is indeed remarkable; the worst,
cluttered, obscure, at times forced or willful rather than
truly imaginative. In spite of the fact that these early
poems take as material what are supposedly universal
conditions of existence, they are often rather private and
restricted by their youthful author's preoccupations.

Thomas admits as much in a later broadcast, "On Reading One's Own Poems," when he speaks of "the very many lives and deaths whether seen, as in my first poems, in the tumultuous world of my own being or, as in the later poems, in war, grief, and the great holes and corners of universal love." Though usually identifiable as a presence in his poetry, whether disguised for dramatic purposes or speaking in his own person, Thomas's attitude toward, and thus his handling of, experience differs markedly in the early work, where all events appear to take place, as it were, within himself and are limited by their subjection to his own inner conflicts and fixed interests, from the later, in which his imagination and linguistic skill fashion a larger poetic universe. Many of the early poems, in spite of their great originality and terrible intensity, suffer from the narrow perspective they impose on experience; the later work achieves an expansiveness of spirit which accepts and transfigures reality, creates, through an increasing wealth and design of language, a poetic myth celebrating the total pattern of life.

Progression toward this final stage of Thomas's poetry is not rapid, nor should we wish it to be, for there are so many excellent poems along the way. In his second book, *25 Poems* (1936), he examines more directly aspects of existence that will ultimately make of him an essentially religious, which is not to say orthodox (in the sense of Eliot or Auden), poet. In fact, he has been a religious poet from the start. Who can doubt it after reading poems whose main concern is cyclical process, human anguish before time and change and death? Now Thomas also confronts the questions of innocence and guilt, the burdens of knowledge, the age-old dilemmas of evil, pain, and tyranny in such poems as "Was there a time," "The hand that signed the paper," "Should lanterns shine," and "Why east wind chills":

> Why east wind chills and south wind cools
> Shall not be known till windwell dries
> And west's no longer drowned
> In winds that bring the fruit and rind
> Of many a hundred falls;
> Why silk is soft and the stone wounds
> The child shall question all his days,
> Why night-time rain and the breast's blood
> Both quench his thirst he'll have a black reply. (62)

Into these lines the poet condenses the riddles of human existence and confesses at the finish that he, like the rest of us, must be kept in doubt until the end of the world as we presently know it ("till windwell dries/And west's no longer drowned"). Here commences an outward turning which brings Thomas to contemplation of events and people within a broader framework of reality. If he is still engaged imaginatively by perennial themes of birth, time, innocence, and death that occupy the major portion of his first poems, his treatment of them has altered to include the richness and joy of life, for all of its tragic limitations, and increasingly to see both personal and collective existence as part of a whole mythic scheme.

What we might call a ritual pattern of life, which comes to its fulfillment in the magnificent celebrations and elegies of Thomas's latest period, supplies a religious resonance to this work. While there is no fundamental change in the harsh actualities of mortal nature, no escape from process, the phases of life are now understood to fit into a kind of archetypal plan starting at birth and concluding in images of resurrection or the hope of paradise. Thomas no longer emphasizes inner biological operations or the secrets of prenatal being; instead he observes human life against the background of the external world, the passing seasons with their legacy of symbolic implications, and, more and more as he proceeds, the landscape of his native Wales. In "And death shall have no dominion" he demonstrates for the first time some elements of his slowly developing mythic vision. The quality of speech and the tone are appropriately exalted, for Thomas's statement is public and prophetic:

> And death shall have no dominion.
> Dead men naked they shall be one
> With the man in the wind and the west moon;
> When their bones are picked clean and the clean bones
>   gone,
> They shall have stars at elbow and foot;
> Though they go mad they shall be sane,
> Though they sink through the sea they shall rise again;
> Though lovers be lost love shall not;
> And death shall have no dominion. (72)

Thomas has adopted his five-times-repeated opening line from St. Paul (Romans 6:9) and in each of the three stanzas depicts the survival of human virtue under attack by various forms of evil. The poem everywhere suggests regeneration or resurrection following the general wave of destructiveness, though again, as in "Why east wind chills," there are hints in the closing portion that the force of evil will only disappear at some far-off, apocalyptic moment:

> Though they be mad and dead as nails,
> Heads of the characters hammer through daisies;

Break in the sun till the sun breaks down,
And death shall have no dominion. (72)

As we said previously, the figure of Christ makes several appearances in Thomas's earlier verse, though there He acts simply as a powerful symbolic representative of man's earthly predicament. We are given no evidence that the poet thinks of Him as more than a unique victim of mortal circumstances, even when occasional details of His divine nature are noticeable, as in "Before I knocked." The famed sonnet sequence, "Alterwise by owl-light," which has been the object of elaborate and ingenious exegesis by such skilled critics as Elder Olson and W. Y. Tindall, however, begins a departure from that previous attitude and explores much more closely the relationship between the poet and Christ. So much about the sequence is clear, though very little else is. One discovers arresting lines and passages, but most of the poems are pointlessly confusing. Both David Daiches and G. S. Fraser have criticized the sequence for a failure to yield enough substantial and consistent meaning to justify itself, and I am in agreement with them. I would add that parts are glib and in poor taste:

And from the windy West came two-gunned Gabriel,
From Jesu's sleeve trumped up the king of spots . . . (82)

But as an example of the best parts here is the eighth sonnet, on the Crucifixion, which has a quality akin to that of some marvelous and inspired medieval painting of the subject. Through the persons of Jesus and Mary the witnessing poet sees time and death absorbed and transcended in this redemptive sacrifice:

This was the crucifixion on the mountain,
Time's nerve in vinegar, the gallow grave
As tarred with blood as the bright thorns I wept;
The world's my wound, God's Mary in her grief,
Bent like three trees and bird-papped through her shift,
With pins for teardrops is the long wound's woman.
This was the sky, Jack Christ, each minstrel angle
Drove in the heaven-driven of the nails
Till the three-colored rainbow from my nipples
From pole to pole leapt round the snail-waked world
I by the tree of thieves, all glory's sawbones,
Unsex the skeleton this mountain minute,
And by this blowclock witness of the sun
Suffer the heaven's children through my heartbeat. (83-84)

The last lines portray Christ as, so to speak, God's doctor ("all glory's sawbones") who, as He dies at this crucial instant in history ("Unsex the skeleton this mountain minute"), dissolves time ("blowclock") and cures all men by including them in His purgative death. The final poem of the sequence brings the quest or, as Thomas calls it, "a Christian voyage" (85), to a finish and offers images of purification and renewal; here we find traditional Christian symbols of Eden, the Tree of Knowledge, and the Satanic worm or serpent of death. Even in this often cluttered and unsuccessful sequence Thomas is working his way toward the mythic conception of the later poetry.

Two other poems pursue the theme of Christ: "There was a Savior" and, most important, "Vision and Prayer." This second piece is Thomas's only attempt to make any statement of mystical or illuminative experience. It is an extremely personal work, really a confessional poem. Like the 17th century religious poet George Herbert he arranges the layout of his poem in the shapes of diamond and hourglass, one for each of the two sections. The first part constitutes the vision; the second, the supplication, with a return to climactic vision at the end. The poem begins with the poet asking the identity of one "Who is born/In the room/So loud to my own/That I can hear the womb/Opening and the dark run/Over the ghost and the dropped son/Behind the wall thin as a wren's bone" (154). Both poet and unknown child lie secure but are waiting for birth. We soon learn that this child is Christ, who, watched by the poet, has His suffering and sacrifice foretold. Yet knowledge of the child's birth also fills the poet with apprehension for another reason; he is required to surrender himself to the absolute demands of Divine love: "I shall run lost in sudden/Terror and shining from/The once hooded room/Crying in vain/ In the caldron/Of his/Kiss" (156). An imagery of intense light, often used by mystical writers to describe such an encounter, continues throughout this section in flames, lightning, "high noon" (156), the sun, and "the shrine/Of his blazing/Breast" (158).

In spite of his terror the poet, who "was lost," reaches a "dumbfounding haven" (157), and in some eloquent lines envisages the redemption of his fallen nature, the restoration of his innocence: "I shall waken/To the judge blown bedlam/Of the uncaged sea bottom/The cloud climb of the exhaling tomb/And the bidden dust up-sailing/With his flame in every grain" (158). This is another instance of that resurrection imagery mentioned before. Submission to Christ results in new life, for the fire of His love purifies and renews; in the last stanza of section one Thomas sees Eden restored: "The/Born sea/Praised the sun/The finding one/And upright Adam/Sang upon origin!" (159). The elements of the universe are again in harmony; those who have endured pain and died are awakened; the visions of saints become tangible reality. Thomas, and such other modern English visionary poets as Edwin Muir and Kathleen Raine, look forward to the abolition of time, the completion of the circle of history, when all creatures and things will be restored to a state of primal innocence and purity —"The world winding home!" (159). At this ecstatic revelation the poet dies to himself in the simultaneous pain of purgation and wonder of vision.

Section II starts with a sense of the exalted character of the preceding vision and its impossible distance from man as he now is. So Thomas turns realist and prays "In the name of the lost who glory in/The swinish plains of carrion" (160)—that is, for those bound to earth by sin and spiritual indifference—that they may re-enter the womb and never know Christ's coming. These sinners and unbelievers should not be led to a redemption beyond their natures but left to the familiar regions of spiritual blindness: "Places/Ways/Mazes/Passages/ Quarters and graves/Of the endless fall" (163). Fallen man has accustomed himself to his estate, so that "the country of death is the heart's size/And the star of the lost the shape of the eyes" (163-164). The prayer closes with a request that Christ's sacrifice appear in this twilight world not for what it was but merely as a human and final death; faith in or knowledge of His resurrection alters reality and means a transformation of human nature. After the prayer there occurs an unexpected answer, "a blessing of the sudden/Sun" (165), which, as

in Section I, causes the poet vainly to flee: "But the
loud sun/Christens down/The sky./I Am found"
(165). And so another time Thomas submits to purgation and assimilation in Christ as the poem concludes:
"O let him/Scald me and drown/Me in his world's
wound./His lightning answers my/Cry. My voice
burns in his hand./Now I am lost in the blinding/One.
The sun roars at the prayer's end" (165). If this ending
exhibits Thomas's sense of the frightening seizure of the
imperfect self by the Divine, it also shows his profound
desire for that embrace.

Elsewhere in his mature poems Thomas maintains the
personal approach to experience evident in "Vision and
Prayer." Three birthday poems, written for his 24th,
30th, and 35th years, place his individual existence in
relation to the pattern of life as a whole. The first,
"Twenty-four Years," investigates the intimate connec-
tions between birth and death. The poet represents himself as both a tailor and a dandy who makes and wears
his outfit, ironically consisting of grave clothes, on a "sen-
sual strut" which leads finally to "the elementary town"
(110) or back to earth again at death. Even though
Thomas refers to the passage of his own life, the poem
is objectively conceived in symbolic figures illustrative
of the relentlessly impersonal movement of process.

By way of contrast, "Poem in October" is more intimate, in the manner of "Vision and Prayer," and yet it also
creates the setting of a mythical Wales, a self-contained
world of the imagination in which is enacted the ritual
drama of existence of the pastoral poems "Fern Hill," "In
Country Sleep," "In the White Giant's Thigh," "Over Sir
John's Hill," "Author's Prologue," and "Poem on his Birth-

day." The prose counterpart to these poems is *Under Milk Wood,* a play for voices which captures the endless round of life in a small Welsh town with that marvelous feeling for comedy and pathos so outstanding in Thomas's later short stories, unfinished novel, and various other prose sketches and memoirs. But the major work of these years remains the poetry, for natural and artistic growth, as well as the terrible lasting impression of the war, elicited some of his finest work ("A Refusal to Mourn," "Ceremony After a Fire Raid," "Among those Killed") and brought both imaginative and technical gifts, augmented by a more mature, reflective cast of mind, to a peak of achievement. "Poem in October" is, then, a personal meditation which avoids the restrictions of autobiography; its interwoven texture of images and metaphors forms a rich, magical creation whose seasons match the temporal stages of the poet's (or anyone's) life. He is encouraged to view its fundamental pattern as a recurrent mythic scheme. Language, here as in other late poems, is decisive in fashioning the reality of this Welsh pastoral scene and sustaining it. While Thomas sought in his early poems to embody the flux of experience in a complex of imagery seized as close as possible to the sources of that experience, now he tries to produce a language which can substantially incorporate the vast abundance of earthly life and re-create it, by the power of words, into sacred legend or parable. In his hands words gain the ability to mythologize, to make sacred. So for Thomas, as for Blake, Hopkins, Lawrence, and Edith Sitwell, creation becomes holy: "It was my thirtieth year to heaven/Woke to my hearing from harbor and neighbor wood/And the mussel pooled and the heron/

Priested shore/The morning beckon/With water praying and call of seagull and rook . . ." (113).

The poem continues with elements of nature participating symbolically in the poet's birthday as he departs from "the still sleeping town" to climb the sunny "hill's shoulder" (113) beyond. In the idyllic countryside he could easily pass this special day "but the weather turned around"; and the poet is granted a momentary vision in which he relives his childhood, enters again a state of innocence and sacredness only to be compared with life before the Fall: "And I saw in the turning so clearly a child's/Forgotten mornings when he walked with his mother/Through the parables/Of sun light /And the legends of the green chapels . . ." (114). His childhood is further pictured as close to a ritual act of prayer, though it is completely unself-conscious, the mode of living in innocence: "a boy/In the listening/ Summertime of the dead whispered the truth of his joy /To the trees and the stones and the fish in the tide./ And the mystery/Sang alive/Still in the water and singingbirds" (115). The poem finishes with the dissolving of vision and a return to the present. Though this pure age of childhood has vanished with time, the poet, by seeking it in his art, revives its lost qualities, sings his "heart's truth" (115), that we may find and experience that world in ourselves.

"Fern Hill" carries the central experience of "Poem in October" to its origin, that is, to the prelapsarian Wales of the young Thomas, and is, if anything, a more complete hymn of praise for life. But the unfallen world this poem presents likewise contains the cause of its undoing, which is always visible though we scarcely notice it

amidst the fine sensuous description of an ideal existence: "Now as I was young and easy under the apple
boughs/About the lilting house and happy as the grass
was green,/The night above the dingle starry,/Time
let me hail and climb/Golden in the heydays of his
eyes,/And honored among wagons I was prince of the
apple towns . . ." (178). The cause is a familiar one,
time, which, we realize as the poem goes on, permits
this happy period "Before the children green and golden
/Follow him out of grace" (179); and once we have
seen this inevitability the "apple towns" and their youthful prince readily suggest a biblical archetype that
Thomas anyway makes explicit: "it was all/Shining, it
was Adam and maiden,/The sky gathered again/And
the sun grew round that very day./So it must have been
after the birth of the simple light/In the first, spinning
place, the spellbound horses walking warm/Out of the
whinnying green stable/On to the fields of praise"
(179). The poem actually moves from a celebration of
this innocent life (though Thomas's use of a past tense
indicates that it no longer exists except in the poem) to
an elegy for its loss. So Thomas has not abandoned his
awareness of mortality, as his magnificent war elegies
also testify, but his basic attitude toward the life cycle
has shifted from one of pessimism, anxiety, and obses-
siveness about biological determinacy to one of religious
exaltation, faith in the value and sanctity of life despite
its harsh conclusion. Moreover, he thinks of his poetry
as a statement of this faith, the incarnation of it in words.
In "Over Sir John's Hill" he praises the lives of a variety
of birds from hawk to sparrows and reads their mortal
term just as he reads his own; at the poem's end he

explains his art as a testament to the dying birds and, by analogy, to his human existence: "I who hear the tune of the slow,/Wear-willow river, grave,/Before the lunge of the night, the notes on this timeshaken/Stone for the sake of the slain birds sailing" (189).

The final "Poem on his Birthday" develops a primary metaphor of voyage or journey, often used by Thomas as indicative of the progression from cradle to grave. Like other late pieces this one opens with the author meditating upon the life of nature he can observe before him. His birthday marks the accomplishment of another portion of his journey toward death, a journey in which he is joined by the creatures he watches: "Curlews aloud in the congered waves/Work at their ways to death,/ And the rhymer in the long tongued room,/Who tolls his birthday bell,/Toils toward the ambush of his wounds . . ." (190). Thinking about the prospect of mortality in general brings him at last to contemplate his own demise and the uncertainty of what will follow. Death is the bursting of a cage and chains, then "love unbolts the dark" and the poet "goes lost" (191) toward God. The geography of paradise seems an extension of sorts of the mythic Wales of "Fern Hill" and other poems, but Thomas's vision does not linger here because "dark is a long way" and he has far to go to attain "old/And air shaped Heaven where souls grow wild/As horses in the foam" (192). Life's "voyage to ruin" must first be seen through to its finish, and it, rather than the ultimate destiny of the self, is the material of poetry.

The closing stanzas once more sing the beauty and miracle of creation, until the thought of death simply enhances the preciousness of existence; the poet sets aside pain and terror for affirmation: "the closer I move/To death, one man through his sundered hulks,/The louder the sun blooms/And the tusked ramshackling sea exults . . ." (193). Such a positive note characterizes the underlying feeling of these last poems commemorating the mortal cycle in which Thomas discovers a plan and fulfillment in man's ancient sacred history. Innocence, the Fall, life in time, and the vision of resurrection provide a mythic or fabulistic pattern with which his work reaches conclusion. In the manner of the greatest English religious poets Thomas has found that pattern through his own experience; the dignity of its artistic expression will keep him alive in the memory of many generations to come.

NOTE

1. Numbers in parentheses following quoted selections in this chapter refer to page numbers in *The Collected Poems of Dylan Thomas*. Copyright 1953 by Dylan Thomas. © 1957 by New Directions. Reprinted by permission of the publishers, New Directions, New York.

IV *Auden's Subject:*

"THE HUMAN CLAY"—
"THE VILLAGE OF THE HEART"

BY NATHAN A. SCOTT, JR.

One of the principal embarrassments in the literary
life of the present time is the general uneasiness that is
felt before the work and unignorable presence of one
who for over thirty years has had to be counted amongst
the major poets of our time. Throughout the nineteen-
thirties it was easily possible to find a place for W. H.
Auden on the map of things as a prodigiously clever
and intelligent young man who had mastered all the difficult lessons of Hopkins and Eliot and Pound and Yeats,
who had a curious capacity for viewing all the disinte-
gration of modern life "as the hawk sees it or the hel-
meted airman"—as a young man who was creating a
new music of his own, who in his poem of 1937 on
"Spain" had created one of the most memorable works
of the time, and who was undeniably a person of great
promise. There was nothing particularly unsettling (at
least for the devotees of the avant-garde) in his public
presence: he was a bright young Englishman who had
gone up to Oxford with people like Stephen Spender and
Cecil Day Lewis, and there he had become a poet, des-

tined apparently to be the most important representative of this literary generation. He had written bluntly,
and sometimes memorably and movingly, about the in-
ternational malaise of the years of *l'entre deux guerres;*
but, though his pen had proven to be a vigorous scalpel
for the probing of the tension and the unrest in "the condemned playground" of the thirties, he was by no means
unassimilable into the fashionable literary culture of the
period. The poet who was brooding upon the massive
taciturnity of this "Age of Ice" and who was envisaging
"New styles of architecture, a change of heart" seemed,
indeed, to be describing the trajectory that had taken its
rise in Pound and the early Eliot and that was to be
completed by his own generation. And when I think
back to the beginning of the forties and to my under-
graduate days in Ann Arbor, where Mr. Auden was then
in residence at the University, my recollection is that the
pale, tousle-headed, briskly striding exile in loafers, with
the loud plaid sport-jacket and khaki trousers, whom we
saw walking about the streets of the town, was for us so
exciting and bracing a figure because he embodied so
much of the *promise* of whatever was to be achieved by
Eliot's successors.

But now in the years that have since intervened, the
poet of *New Year Letter, The Sea and the Mirror, For
the Time Being,* and *The Age of Anxiety* has drawn a
circle of definition about himself that has revealed the
coherence, the inner complication, and the profundity of
his vision of human life—and that has established him
not simply as a figure of promise but as one of the major
strategists of modern poetry. Yet there is still today a
strange irritation that overtakes criticism, when his

achievement comes into view. And one gets the impression from the tone in which he is sometimes talked about that, notwithstanding the conventional acknowledgments of his importance, he is really something of a cark and a botheration.

This disaffiliation of the last twenty years or so between Mr. Auden and his public may be a result of the fact that, as he has entered more and more deeply into the Christian understanding of human existence, the nature of his dedication to the life of poetry has itself undergone great transformation—so that since, say, 1940, the desire that has stirred his poetry into life has been not merely that of *exposing* the disorder and dilapidation of modern life (as in the thirties) but, rather, that of stretching the secular mind of our period to the very limits of its memory, the limits beyond which there remains nothing for it to know but the foolishness of many of its wise men and the illusoriness of many of the myths by means of which it has attempted to reckon with modern history. His descent has been into the social, the political, the religious, the ideological confusions of our time. And, though he has his special allegiances to Dante and Pascal and Kierkegaard and to thinkers like Barth and Niebuhr in the contemporary period, his mind has been alert to the entire European tradition (the Greeks, the Church Fathers, the medieval Scholastics, the Reformers, Spinoza, Blake, Voltaire, Baudelaire, Rimbaud, Nietzsche, Wagner, Freud, and so on), and it is its immense pressure that he seeks to bring to bear upon the predicaments of modern life. So his poetry has often been an embarrassment to those critical orthodoxies of the present which represent the poem, generi-

cally, as an ironic pattern of reflexive verbal gestures
that makes no clean statement about anything at all. Mr.
Auden's mind (to invert that famous sexual metaphor of
Eliot's about Henry James) has not been unwilling to be
violated by ideas, his verse is chock full of them: indeed,
it is a poetry of argument, a poetry of discussion, and
—like Pope and Wordsworth and Yeats and Eliot himself and most of those whose poetry has become a permanent part of the furniture of our minds—his way of
enacting his vocational role has, to some extent, been
that of the rhetorician. This has been his delight and also
his burden, the expense of which is discernible precisely
in the resistance that his methods have provoked in
many readers.

Given the emphatically secular bias which prevails in
the forums of our cultural life, what has no doubt been
most unsettling in Mr. Auden's career is the radically
Christian judgments upon modern life which his mind and
his art have embraced. To put this construction upon
the malice that has so frequently figured in critical discussion of his work is, of course, to invite, as a rejoinder,
the question as to why it is—if Mr. Auden's difficulties
with the judicial process of modern criticism are the consequence of a collision in the realm of belief—that such
a writer as the late T. S. Eliot did not have to endure
similar difficulties. And, when this question is raised, it
must immediately be countered that, indeed, for a time
he did, as will be revealed by even a casual inspection
of much of the criticism devoted to his work during
the thirties. But, of course, it must be admitted that, at
the time of his death in 1964, he had been for twenty-
five years the most universally honored figure in the

literary community. And I think that this was possible (despite the many respects in which his own thought was equally as subversive of modern secularism as Mr. Auden's) because *The Waste Land*—which was the climatic expression of the earlier phase of his career—has long been responded to more often as a document than as a great modern poem. That is to say, one feels that it is cherished as the poem that made a genuinely modern poetry possible, by disclosing how the fragmentariness of modern life might be encompassed by the poetic imagination—which means that, insofar as it is so responded to today, our sense of the history of modern poetry has partially neutralized those elements of Eliot's parable that might otherwise be expected to have a nettling effect and has distanced us from their inquisitorial power. As for the poetry of his later, explicitly Christian phase, it did of course, after *Ash Wednesday,* tend to skirt the embroilments of contemporary ideology for the sake of scanning that highly private *askesis* which the soul must undertake for the recovery of its own integrity and for the apprehension of that Moment which is "in time and of time . . . transecting, bisecting the world of time," yet "not like a moment of time," because, in being the Moment of the Incarnation, it is the Moment which gave to time its meaning. And it has been possible for secular intellectuals to regard all this as something very "special" which Eliot was to be allowed, his mind having taken the idiosyncratic and archaistic turn that it did— just as Yeats was to have been allowed his lunar phases and towers and spiral staircases and Pound his passion for the economics of Major C. H. Douglas and Silvio Gesell.

The great point, however, is that the way in which it is necessary for Mr. Auden to use his Christian beliefs as a poet is a way that inevitably involved his forfeiting this kind of permissiveness. He tells us, for example, in his "Christmas Oratorio" that

> . . . the garden is the only place there is, but you will not find it
> Until you have looked for it everywhere and found nowhere that is not a desert. (412)[1]

And, believing this as profoundly as he does, he has, therefore, had to relate himself to modern culture in a way that has permitted some to regard his career as representing mere adventurism in the realm of ideas. But this is the worldliness, and the greatness, of Mr. Auden's mind: it is a mind for which acceptance of the scandal of Christianity is possible only after every alternative to the Christian faith has been faced and evaluated, only after all the other great ways of dealing with the human problem have been explored and tested against the basic realities of human experience. All the wrong roads must be traveled, so that, finally, when the right road is found, should we stumble again into some blind detour, it may be recognized for what it is. And this being the habit of his mind, Mr. Auden has, therefore, faced the whole repertoire of beliefs and philosophies, of programs and ideologies, that the modern world has conceived: though a pilgrim, he has, at the same time, been an explorer who has covered the entire terrain that is accessible to the men of his age. And that he should have negotiated *such* an odyssey and *then* chosen to give his suffrage to the Christian faith!—this it is that has, I believe, so profoundly scandalized his

contemporaries, and done so to a far greater degree than
the religious orthodoxy of such men as Claudel and
Mauriac, who could be regarded as living at a much
greater remove from modern experience and whose faith
could, therefore, in a way, be accepted as, in some measure, a consequence of their isolation.

It is true, of course, that to some extent his progress
(as Randall Jarrell suggested, in a bilious estimate of
Mr. Auden's achievement in the mid-forties[2]) has been
from Marx and Freud to Paul, though no absolute dis-
junction can, I think, be established between the outlook
embodied in the earlier poetry and that which informs
the work of the past twenty-five years. The young poet
who entered the literary life of England in 1930 with the
slender volume entitled *Poems* had come into maturity
in a world that seemed everywhere to bear the marks
of seediness and decay. The economic system had lapsed
into an extreme depression: men were without employ-
ment and were hungry and had no hope: everywhere
there was confusion and dismay. It was, as Mr. Auden
said in poem XXII of his first book, a time of

> Smokeless chimneys, damaged bridges, rotting wharves
>   and choked canals,
> Tramlines buckled, smashed trucks lying on their side
>   across the rails.
> Power-stations locked, deserted . . . (P. 39)

But what is clear in this first volume is that he was not
only sensitively aware of the breakdown of the social
and economic machinery but that he was already aware
of the deeper symptoms of the crisis. For, unlike the
orthodox leftists of the period who could so precisely
locate the root of the malaise in the social-economic

structure, he turned to the insecurity of the individual and to the bleak, dreary winter of his isolateness:

> So, insecure, he loves and love
> Is insecure, gives less than he expects.
> He knows not if it be seed in time to display
> Luxuriantly in a wonderful fructification
> Or whether it be but a degenerate remnant
> Of something immense in the past but now
> Surviving only as the infectiousness of disease . . .
> (P. 30)

And the consistency with which he portrayed (not only in *Poems* of 1930 but in all the work of the decade—in the charade *Paid on Both Sides,* in *The Orators,* in *The Dance of Death,* in the plays with Christopher Isherwood, in *On This Island,* and in *Another Time*) the human individual as living at a point of juncture between *both* the public world of society and the inner world of the psyche represented an attitude itself already inclinatorily Christian. For secular sociologism has tended to regard the inner life of the psyche as merely an epiphenomenon dependent upon forces and structures that are of an essentially social nature—whereas the psychologies descending from Freud have tended to minimize, if not to ignore, the social determination of personality. So, though Mr. Auden was attracted to both perspectives, he seems already in the thirties to have defined a point of view of his own, and one that, in absorbing *both* Marxist *and* Freudian perspectives, looked forward to the Christian emphasis upon man's creaturely involvement in the concrete stuff of social history and upon the essential interiority of his existence, its irreducibility to the epiphenomena of the social collective.

The constant stress, then, that grows out of this double focus and that figures very largely in Mr. Auden's poetry throughout the thirties is that which fell, in his very first book, upon *both* "new styles of architecture" *and* "a change of heart."

Increasingly, however, Mr. Auden's interest, throughout the period, came more and more to center not so much upon the problems arising out of the mechanics of our social living as upon what he took to be the ultimate and habitual source of these problems, in the crookedness and illiberality of the human heart. And in his two finest books of the decade—*On This Island* and *Another Time*—what he is seeking to throw a searchlight upon in poem after poem is the general failure of love. "We have fallen apart/Into the isolated personal life." And it is no wonder "so many die of grief,/So many are so lonely as they die." As he puts it in poem XXX of *On This Island,*

> . . . the word is love
> Surely one fearless kiss would cure
> The million fevers . . .

The "nervous" headache and the ugly rash, the pain in the side and the bitten fingernails may, in other words, be the symptoms of an inner disobedience that "makes our private bodies ill": to refuse to love may, indeed, be to die: this is the persistently recurrent refrain of *Poems* (1930), of *The Orators* (1932), of *On This Island* (1936), and of *Another Time* (1940). The focus is on the "civil anarchy" that rules our "dark disordered city," and the poetry moves toward the recognition expressed in the last chorus of *The Ascent of F6*, that, yes,

> . . . Love finally is great,
> Greater than all: but large the hate
> Far larger than man can ever estimate.

It is in the *New Year Letter* of 1940 that we get a summary of all that Mr. Auden had learned in the nineteen-thirties. It is perhaps the finest expression to be found anywhere in his work of the belief to which he has held throughout his career, that "we are conscripts to our age"; and, above all else, it records the poet's conviction that "A day is drawing to a close . . . That all the special tasks begun/By the Renaissance have been done" (301). The technical facility of the *Letter* does at times represent extraordinary distinction, and it is undoubtedly true that the masterful use which Mr. Auden here makes of the old convention of the rhymed couplet and the quadruply stressed iambic line has the effect of disclosing one way in which it may perhaps still be possible in our time for the long poem to be written. The language is, to be sure, here and there, marred by his incorrigible penchant for joking and a brittle sort of insouciance; the conversational rhythms of his syntax are occasionally the source of an unfortunate flaccidity of tone; and he is sometimes betrayed by the very exuberance of his genius for epigrammatic statement into merely cataloguing arresting epithets. But, on the whole, his speech is marked by a simplicity, a plainness, a vigor, that make it a wonderfully flexible instrument to

> Disturb our negligence and chill,
> Convict our pride of its offence
> In all things, even penitence,
> Instruct us in the civil art
> Of making from the muddled heart

A desert and a city where
The thoughts that have to labour there
May find locality and peace,
And pent-up feelings their release . . . (315)

It is, indeed, in the *New Year Letter* that Mr. Auden's
vision gains perhaps its most concentrated definition, and
it is, I believe, the central example of his art.

The poem addresses itself to "the situation of our
time," to the "political upheaval" with which "our lives
have been coeval." For Mr. Auden's generation this has,
of course, been an upheaval that has involved, first, the
sudden mutation of "Old Russia . . . /Into a proletarian
state" that gave birth to the most ardent hopes for
man's future that this century has known—and, then, the
discovery by the liberal conscience of the intolerable
moral ambiguities that were necessitated by the inner
logic of the new system. And this has been the central
drama of recent spiritual history because there is none
other that more fully illumines the illusionism in our
time about human existence that has been so deeply em-
bedded in the culture of secular liberalism—whose wise
men for so long persuaded us to believe that there is
some simple path to felicity, either by way of science or
education or universal suffrage. But, increasingly, the
democratic idealism of the eighteenth and nineteenth
centuries proved itself to be incapable of making sense
of the gross and stubborn inequalities in the technocratic
civilization of the modern age. For, even if you do equal-
ize political power, how can you have social justice if the
significant economic power remains in the hands of an
elite that is unresponsive to the common good? And,
even if you do widely extend the literacy of your citizens,

what possibility really exists of their withstanding oppression, if the organs which shape public opinion are in the hands of their oppressors?

It was the apparent inability, then, of the traditional democratic faith to furnish realistic answers to questions such as these which led the liberal mind in the twenties and thirties to become increasingly disillusioned about the moral resources of Western democracy. Yet, having been so deeply habituated in the belief that "the human mind could ultimately arbitrate all competing interests and eliminate all conflict" and "that there is a simple path to universal justice and harmony,"[3] secular liberalism could very easily progress from a democratic to a Marxian utopianism, and to the conviction that the single source of all friction and injustice in the human community is disproportionate economic power. Thus it was that in our period the earlier scriptures of Smith and Spencer and Comte were replaced by the revelations of Marx, and, with the rise of the Russian experiment,

> Some dreamed, as students always can,
> It realized the potential Man,
> A higher species brought to birth
> Upon a sixth part of the earth . . . (285)

At last it seemed that the Rights of Man were about to be enacted into existence in the great Convention of the Proletariat:

> We hoped: we waited for the day
> The State would wither clean away,
> Expecting the Millennium
> That theory promised us would come,
> It didn't. Specialists must try
> To detail all the reasons why . . . (288)

And not only did the earlier promises fail to be realized:
nay, even more: to the utter bafflement of the liberal
mind, this "People's Democracy" proved itself to be an
oligarchy quite as ruthless and tyrannical as the Nazi
oligarchy, and far more dangerous, since, instead of being absolutely cynical, it is rooted in a principled self-
righteousness which enables it to pose as the protagonist
of Justice and which, at the same time, renders it immune
to every effort at moral suasion from without. So it is no
wonder, then, that

> ... even the best,
> *Les hommes de bonne volonté,* feel
> Their politics perhaps unreal
> And all they have believed untrue,
> Are tempted to surrender to
> The grand apocalyptic dream ... (273)

But "to surrender to/The grand apocalyptic dream,"
to abdicate from history and to elect that it shall come to
an end—this is precisely what the Devil desires, for ab-
dication is confession of defeat. Or, if he cannot manage
this, he'll call

> ... at breakfast in the rôle
> Of blunt but sympathetic soul:
> "Well, how's our Socialist this morning? ...
> I'll fix you something for your liver."
> And thus he sells us down the river.
> Repenting of our last infraction
> We seek atonement in reaction ... (289)

This happened to poor Wordsworth, who, after seeing
"in the fall of the Bastille/The Parousia of liberty,"
when "Left by Napoleon in the lurch,"

> . . . ended as the Devil knew
> An earnest Englishman would do . . .
> Supporting the Established Church,
> The Congress of Vienna and
> The Squire's paternalistic hand. (284-285)

But, in a time of shattered dreams and broken hopes, to surrender either to apocalypticism or to reactionism is to withdraw from the rough, dark weathers of history—and, if we do this, then we shall never find "a sesame to light."

Now, says Mr. Auden, "There are two atlases: the one /The public space where acts are done,/In theory common to us all" (296), and it is to the definition of this outer space, in terms of the modern experience, that Parts I and II of the *Letter* are devoted. But then there is the other,

> . . . the inner space
> Of private ownership, the place
> That each of us is forced to own,
> Like his own life from which it's grown,
> The landscape of his will and need
> Where he is sovereign indeed,
> The state created by his acts
> Where he patrols the forest tracts
> Planted in childhood, farms the belt
> Of doings memorized and felt,
> And even if he find it hell
> May neither leave it nor rebel. (296-297)

And it is to the exploration of this inner landscape that a main part of Section III of the poem is devoted, for Mr. Auden has always believed that you do not have disorder in the City when there is order in the private lives of individuals and that the ultimate source of the collective distress is, therefore, to be found in "the error bred in the bone/Of each woman and each man." This is why one of the unifying themes of all his poetry is the call for "a change of heart," and this explains that tendency of his verse (so often noted by his critics) to break out into prayers of petition and intercession: for him the ultimate drama is enacted by the will as it wrestles with itself in the moment of moral choice.

The "two atlases," in other words—"the public space" and "the inner space"—overlap each other in Mr. Auden's thought: so the latter part of the *Letter* wants to make us understand that, if we would be conscripted to our age and become true "patriots of the Now," we must canvass the entire history of the modern period. For, given the essential historicity of man's life—the fact that the individual is in large part "the result of that which he himself and others before him have been and done and thought, of historical decisions that cannot be revoked"[4]—there is no other way in which man can proceed to actualize his humanity except that which involves a stock-taking of the roots in collective experience from which he is sprung. And, when the modern past is examined, the inescapable lesson that must be pondered, says Mr. Auden, is that

> A day is drawing to a close . . .
> That all the special tasks begun
> By the Renaissance have been done. (301)

The "grapevine rumour" prophesying doom to "Empiric Economic Man" that, "at the very noon and arch/Of his immense triumphal march," arose from the mutterings of prophets like Blake and Kierkegaard and Baudelaire has now come true. This new *Anthropos* produced by the

Renaissance and the Enlightenment, who once felt so free in his "splendid isolation" as he drove "himself about creation/In the closed cab of Occupation," is today "captured by his liberty," and

> Whichever way we turn, we see . . .
> The measurable taking charge
> Of him who measures . . .
> The beggar put out by his bowl,
> Boys trained by factories for leading
> Unusual lives as nurses, feeding
> Helpless machines, girls married off
> To typewriters, old men in love
> With prices they can never get,
> Homes blackmailed by a radio set,
> Children inherited by slums
> And idiots by enormous sums. (304)

Yet all these "failures have one good result:/They prove the Good is difficult." Amidst the terrible depersonalization of life in the modern world that has been accomplished by the machine, we can at least discover once again that

> Aloneness is man's real condition,
> That each must travel forth alone
> In search of the Essential Stone . . . (311)

And though (remember: the setting of the poem is New Year's Eve, 1940)—as "Day breaks upon the world we know/Of war and wastefulness and woe"—"The New Year brings an earth afraid," there is one great thing that we are coming once again to understand, that ". . . true democracy begins/With free confession of our sins."

Then the poem concludes with the great prayer—

O Unicorn among the cedars,
To whom no magic charm can lead us . . .
O Dove of science and of light,
Upon the branches of the night . . .
O sudden Wind that blows unbidden,
Parting the quiet reeds, O Voice
Within the labyrinth of choice
Only the passive listener hears,
O Clock and Keeper of the years,
O Source of equity and rest . . .
Disturb our negligence and chill . . .
Send strength sufficient for our day,
And point our knowledge on its way,
O da quod jubes, Domine. (315)

Here, now, we have before us, in the *New Year Letter*, what is, I believe, the definitive statement of Mr. Auden's vision, and his greatest poem—which is, I take it, to say that it is one of the great poems of the modern period. Much of the work that he has produced in the intervening years represents achievement of a very high order, and it is unfortunate that in a brief essay this body of writing cannot be given proper attention. Though in portions of *The Age of Anxiety* (1947) we get a probing of the dislocations and distempers of modern life that goes as deep down as any poet of our period has ventured, I find the greater part of the poem to be life-less and dull. The almost incredible competence that the work exemplifies in the management of alliterative devices represents a degree of technical virtuosity that is not, I suspect, to be matched in any other poet today who is using the English language, and, here and there, one comes upon some remarkably beautiful passages—as, for example, in Rosetta's song "Deep in my dark the dream shines" or Malin's final speech in the Epilogue ("We belong to our kind,/Are judged as we judge . . ."). Yet, on the whole, the poem is controlled by a kind of abstractionism that is quite without the fierce intensity of the *Letter* and that I do not find attractive. But *The Sea and the Mirror* (1945), the Christmas Oratorio *For the Time Being* (1944), and many of the poems in *Nones* (1951) and *The Shield of Achilles* (1955) and *Homage to Clio* (1960) present triumphs of Mr. Auden's art, and I regret the necessity of scanting them on this occasion.

But the measure of the shape and slant of Mr. Auden's mind is still best taken from the *New Year Letter,* and, here, it is revealed as a mind that has consented to expose itself to all the tension and the unrest of the modern world and whose way of arriving at a traditional religious faith has been one leading through all the disarray and confusion of the time. This is why it is a mind whose posture is so secure, and this is why it is so talented in controlling the fragmentariness of modern experience into new patterns of order.

The "patterns of order" which Mr. Auden's imagination has been envisaging since 1940 have been those which thinkers like Kierkegaard and Reinhold Niebuhr and Paul Tillich have assisted him in discovering in the Christian faith, for this is where he has come to find the profoundest clues for the unravelment of the human mystery. But, much as his poetry has gained in depth and complexity as a result of this movement of his mind, it yet shows the signs of the strain that has been exacted of him and that will, I suspect, be required of every writer in our time who attempts to negotiate the odyssey of faith, notwithstanding the erosion of the religious terrain. His friend Stephen Spender has remarked that, despite Mr. Auden's profound "knowledge of the human heart" and his "great gifts of understanding and sympathy," his poetry "lacks respect for the irredeemable mystery of a concrete reality which is inseparable from the nature of things in themselves."[5] And it is true that almost nowhere in Mr. Auden's poetry does he simply *stare* and *look* at the created world, in amazement and expectancy and adoration and praise. The mood that is so magnificently represented, for example, by these lines from one of Wordsworth's sonnets—

> It is a beauteous evening, calm and free,
> The holy time is quiet as a Nun
> Breathless with adoration; the broad sun
> Is sinking down in its tranquility;
> The gentleness of heaven broods o'er the Sea:
> Listen! the mighty Being is awake,
> And doth with his eternal motion make
> A sound like thunder . . .[6]

—this is a mood that is generally quite absent from Mr. Auden's verse. For he is so bent upon wresting a humanly profitable meaning out of the brokenness of modern life that the attitude of amazed and celebratory contemplation (which is surely one of the great attitudes of the mind, and particularly of the Christian imagination, as it confronts the created universe) is one that he very rarely finds it possible to afford. "His poetry," says Mr. Spender, "at times produces the impression that he uses a poetic language to assist himself in the search for a formula which would explain the nature of life."[7]

We are here up against something, however, which is

not, I think, so much an indictment of Mr. Auden as it is an evidence of how expensive for any poet in our period is the mythical vacuum in which we all live. For, in a time when the ultimate frontiers of the human condition are in question, all sensitive men are initiates in the alchemy of spiritual disorientation. And thus it is that the hunger for meaning leads the poet to seek, at whatever cost, to fuse the heterogeneities of experience into some sort of unity: the circumstances of his time make him captive to that mode of the imagination's functioning which Coleridge called "esemplastic." Or he is delivered over, if not to the "esemplastic" imagination, to what Professor Philip Wheelwright calls the "archetypal imagination," whose tendency is to see the particular object or event "as embodying and adumbrating suggestions of universality."[8] And what cannot but be immediately obvious to even Mr. Auden's most cursory readers is that in these two uses of the imagination he possesses the most extraordinary adeptness in contemporary poetry. But when Mr. Spender remarks his impatience with "the irredeemable mystery of . . . concrete reality," his intention, I take it, is to remind us that there are other modes of the imagination's functioning beside the "esemplastic" and the "archetypal" and that (as Professor Wheelwright puts it)

> Poetry's first urgency is, in Richard Hovey's words, to "have business with the grass"; it presents as well as represents, it evokes something of the very quality, tone, and flavor of the concrete *qua* concrete with a directness and a full experiential relevance that steno-symbols cannot do. Authentic poetry will always have this attribute to some degree, for—to paraphrase Yeats—poetry is love, and only the concrete is loved.[9]

Saint Teresa tells us, "I require of you only to look," and this is surely a major imperative for the poet. But in our day, when he has looked out upon the world, what he has seen has impelled him to envisage some better condition for the human spirit, and whatever has offered itself as either sign or vestigial remnant of this has been seized upon as a possible aid in the reconstitution of life —which is to say that his instruments have been the metaphor and the archetype. Were Mr. Spender, however, to generalize the particular observation that he makes on Mr. Auden, he would doubtless want to argue that there are powers of the imagination other than those brought into play by these instruments and that their desuetude entails an impoverishing expense for the poetic enterprise. But, given the special circumstances of our time, this is, I think, an expense that we ought to be glad Mr. Auden has been unafraid to incur, for the result is that, to our very great profit, we have been given a body of poetry which (as F. R. Leavis says of Henry James) has "*added* something as only genius can."[10]

NOTES

1. Numbers in parentheses following quotations indicate page numbers in *The Collected Poetry of W. H. Auden,* published 1945 by Random House, Inc. Used by permission. Quotations from Auden's *Poems,* published 1934 by Random House, Inc., are indicated by P. and used by permission.
2. *Vide* Randall Jarrell, "Freud to Paul: The Stages of Auden's Ideology," *Partisan Review,* Vol. XII, No. 4 (Fall 1945), pp. 437-457.
3. Reinhold Niebuhr, *Christianity and Power Politics* (New York: Charles Scribner's Sons, 1940), p. 54.

4. Erich Frank, *Philosophical Understanding and Religious Truth* (New York: Oxford University Press, 1945), p. 116.

5. Stephen Spender, *Poetry Since 1939* (London: The British Council; published by Longmans, Green and Co., 1946), p. 30.

6. *Poems of William Wordsworth* (New York: Thomas Y. Crowell Company, 1964), p. 93.

7. Spender, *op. cit.*

8. Philip Wheelwright, *The Burning Fountain* (Bloomington: Indiana University Press, 1954), p. 78. The entire chapter (Chapter IV, "Four Ways of Imagination") which Professor Wheelwright devotes to his discussion of the imagination is one of the great sections of this remarkable book.

9. *Ibid.*, p. 79.

10. F. R. Leavis, *The Great Tradition* (London: Chatto and Windus, 1950), p. 16.

SELECTED BIBLIOGRAPHY

A substantial body of the work of Robert Frost and Wallace Stevens is currently available in inexpensive paperback editions—in *The Pocket Book of Robert Frost's Poems,* ed. by Louis Untermeyer (New York: Washington Square Press), and in Wallace Stevens' *Poems,* ed. by Samuel French Morse (New York: Vintage Books). Frost's *Complete Poems* . . . and his other volumes are published by Holt, Rinehart and Winston; and Stevens' *Collected Poems* and his other volumes are published by Alfred A. Knopf. *The Collected Poetry of W. H. Auden* and Mr. Auden's other volumes are published by Random House; and *The Collected Poems of Dylan Thomas* and Thomas's other volumes are published by New Directions.

The following critical studies are recommended:

STEVENS

Marie Boroff, ed., *Wallace Stevens: A Collection of Critical Essays.* Englewood Cliffs, N. J.: Prentice-Hall, Inc., 1963.

Ashley Brown and Robert S. Haller, eds., *The Achievement of Wallace Stevens.* Philadelphia: J. P. Lippincott Co., 1962.

John Jacob Enck, *Wallace Stevens: Images and Judgments.* Carbondale, Ill.: Southern Illinois University Press, 1964.

Daniel Fuchs, *The Comic Spirit of Wallace Stevens.* Durham, N. C.: Duke University Press, 1963.

Frank Kermode, *Wallace Stevens.* Edinburgh: Oliver & Boyd, 1960.

William Van O'Connor, *The Shaping Spirit: A Study of Wallace Stevens.* Chicago: Henry Regnery Co., 1950.

Robert Pack, *Wallace Stevens: An Approach to His Poetry*

and Thought. New Brunswick, N. J.: Rutgers University Press, 1958.

Henry W. Wells, *Introduction to Wallace Stevens.* Bloomington: Indiana University Press, 1964.

FROST

Reuben A. Brower, *The Poetry of Robert Frost: Constellations of Intention.* New York: Oxford University Press, 1963.

Reginald L. Cook, *The Dimensions of Robert Frost.* New York: Holt, Rinehart and Winston, Inc., 1958.

James M. Cox, ed., *Robert Frost: A Collection of Critical Essays.* Englewood Cliffs, N. J.: Prentice-Hall, Inc., 1962.

Elizabeth Jennings, *Frost.* Edinburgh: Oliver & Boyd, 1964.

John F. Lynen, *The Pastoral Art of Robert Frost.* New Haven: Yale University Press, 1960.

Roy Harvey Pearce, "Frost's Momentary Stay," *Kenyon Review,* XXIII (Spring 1961), pp. 258-273.

Elizabeth Shepley Sergeant, *Robert Frost: Trial by Existence.* New York: Holt, Rinehart and Winston, Inc., 1960. A biographical study.

Lawrance Thompson, *Robert Frost.* Minneapolis: University of Minnesota Press, 1959 (University of Minnesota Pamphlets on American Writers, No. 2).

THOMAS

G. S. Fraser, *Dylan Thomas.* London: Longmans, Green & Co., 1957.

T. H. Jones, *Dylan Thomas.* New York: Grove Press, 1963.

H. Kleinman, *The Religious Sonnets of Dylan Thomas: A Study in Imagery and Meaning.* Berkeley: University of California Press, 1963.

Ralph Maud, *Entrances to Dylan Thomas's Poetry.* Pittsburgh: University of Pittsburgh Press, 1963.

Elder Olson, *The Poetry of Dylan Thomas.* Chicago: University of Chicago Press, 1954.

Derek Stanford, *Dylan Thomas*. New York: Citadel Press, 1964.

William York Tindall, *A Reader's Guide to Dylan Thomas*. New York: Noonday Press, 1962.

AUDEN

Joseph Warren Beach, *The Making of the Auden Canon*. Minneapolis: University of Minnesota Press, 1957.

Richard Hoggart, *Auden: An Introductory Essay*. London: Chatto and Windus, 1951.

Moritz Rosenthal, *The Modern Poets: An Introduction*. New York: Oxford University Press, 1955.

R. M. Roth, "The Sophistication of W. H. Auden: A Sketch in Longinian Method," *Modern Philology*, XLVIII (February 1951), pp. 193-204.

Francis Scarfe, *W. H. Auden*. Monaco: The Lyrebird Press, 1949.

Nathan A. Scott, Jr., "The Poetry of Auden," *The Chicago Review*, XIII (Winter 1959), pp. 53-75. Also published in *The London Magazine*, VIII (January 1961), pp. 44-63.

Monroe K. Spears, *The Poetry of W. H. Auden: The Disenchanted Island*. New York and London: Oxford University Press, 1963.

Monroe K. Spears, ed., *Auden: A Collection of Critical Essays*. Englewood Cliffs, N. J.: Prentice-Hall, Inc., 1964.